GLORIOUS

MY WORLD, FOOTBALL AND ME

PAUL GASCOIGNE

GLORIOUS

MY WORLD, FOOTBALL AND ME

WITH DAVID WILSON

SIMON &
SCHUSTER

London · New York · Sydney · Toronto · New Delhi

A CBS COMPANY

First published in Great Britain by Simon & Schuster UK Ltd, 2011
A CBS Company

1 3 5 7 9 10 8 6 4 2

Simon & Schuster UK Ltd
1st Floor
222 Gray's Inn Road
London
WC1X 8HB

www.simonandschuster.co.uk

Simon & Schuster Australia
Sydney
Simon & Schuster India
New Delhi

A CIP catalogue record for this book is available from the British Library

ISBN 978-0-85720-448-6

Design by Nick Venables
Cover design by Matthew Johnson
Printed and bound in Italy by L.E.G.O. SpA

To all you fans who came out to watch.
You made everything worthwhile.
I love you.

CONTENTS

WHAT FOOTBALL MEANS TO ME

Football, fucking hell. I think that's what Sir Alex Ferguson said. Something like that. It sums up my life and it's what this book is all about: my football career, and it has been a belter. I think so anyway. Everything's here. The good, the bad and sometimes the ugly. Me most memorable moments on the pitch, and just occasionally off it.

Come to think about it, maybe I've got that wrong. Perhaps Sir Alex said, 'Gascoigne, fucking hell,' when I didn't sign for Manchester United in the summer of 1988. But that's a story for later.

What has football meant to me? The world, literally. It has taken me across the planet to Albania, Italy, Poland, Hong Kong and I've loved every moment of it. Almost every moment, anyway... I've been to loads of different, fascinating places which I would never have seen otherwise. I've been incredibly lucky, I know that, but I've worked hard too. I was given a talent, perhaps by God, but I trained me arse off to make the most of it. Just ask any manager, coach, or team-mate I played with. Pre-season I'd be there, desperate to get fit and get going again. Mid-week training? They'd have to drag me away! I loved playing football. It was my life and I wanted to be the best I could possibly be.

Some of the stuff I did on a football pitch, I didn't know how I was doing it. I used to feel sorry for defenders because if I didn't have a clue what I was going to do, how the hell were they meant to? Bit unfair really. I just seemed to know instinctively what was ahead of me, who was around me and exactly where the next pass should go.

'I loved playing football. It was my life and I wanted to be the best I could possibly be.'

There has been a downside though, a big one. I am an alcoholic. I know that. I've accepted the fact and I am trying hard, really hard, to beat it once and for all. And I will, even though I know I'll be facing the battle for the rest of me life. But that's okay, as I've already said, I don't mind hard work. I sometimes wonder if I was born to be an alcoholic but I don't think so. I believe I turned to drink because it gave me a release from the pressure of football. I am not using that as an excuse, I am just trying to show how much football meant to me, how obsessed I was by it, and how sometimes that obsession had a negative effect. There were of course millions of other things I could have done to help meself, but I chose drink. Daft.

I used to get angry with myself if I didn't play well. Not that I had that feeling very often, you understand. But when it did happen I would become very low. I wouldn't say depressed, but definitely low. It was another reason to reach for a bottle. The drink would help stop me going over and over in me head the things I had done wrong in the match. But mainly all I wanted to do was get back out there and play better. I couldn't wait for the days to fly past until the next game.

What made it even worse was that when I had a blinding game I still piled the pressure on myself because I was desperate to play as well in the next match, or even better if I could. If I scored a hat trick I used to worry about how the hell I would score another one. That was mental. I should just have been pleased I'd scored, because I wasn't really a striker. I was more of a supplier from midfield. Any goals should have been a bonus not a burden, but that's not how my mind works. If I scored from thirty yards then the next week I had to score from forty.

Even still, with all that pressure I put myself under, and the low points I suffered throughout my career, I still managed to grab a fair few cracking goals and most of them are here in this book. What a laugh it has been reminding meself of some of them. Poor old Shilts and Dave Seaman.

'If I scored a hat trick I used to worry about how the hell I would score another one. That was mental.'

Football not only brought me the world, it paid me well too. That was great, don't get me wrong, but that was never really what it was about for me. If money had been something I really cared about I would have a hell of a lot more now than I do, but I always tried to enjoy the experiences and the privileges I had from football with as many people as I could. That's really why I wanted to do this book, to share some of my favourite football moments (and one or two I'd like to forget) with anyone who might be interested. I hope some of you are, and that it isn't just Mam, Dad, my brother, sisters and me mate Jimmy Gardner (you might know him as Jimmy Five Bellies).

Making connections with fans was always what it was about for me. I never turned down an autograph, photo or a chat with a stranger about the game. I don't think I did anyway. If anyone reading this now knows differently, I am sorry. You must have caught me on a really bad day and I apologise. I was always aware, Mam and Dad made sure I was, that it was the fans turning up in the pissing rain or the freezing snow who paid my wages and I wanted to give as much back as I could – entertain as much as possible – even for the away fans. So I would do mad things sometimes, just for a laugh. I remember in one game I put the ball past the defender, went round him, and carried on running, leaving the ball on the pitch and diving into the crowd. It made everyone laugh. Well, apart from me manager and team-mates. In football today there isn't enough of that sort of thing going on. It's a shame really.

Doing this book has brought loads back to me. Memorable matches, great goals, lucky goals, funny stories, fabulous players. And some disappointments and things I wish I hadn't done, or had done differently. I haven't been able to include everything – the book would be a thousand pages long if I had. So I've narrowed down the hundreds of great memories to the ones I think best illustrate what it was all about for me.

I hope you have as much fun reading it as I have had putting it together.

CHAPTER 1

FIVE MORE MINUTES

DUNSTON:
DECEMBER 1974 – MAY 1983

Football daft. That was me. I was given me first football as a birthday present when I was seven. Before then I'd only ever played with a tennis ball, knocking it against a wall in the playground or out in the street. When I was eventually given a proper ball, I found playing with it a doddle. That tennis ball probably helped shape me career.

I loved that football. It never left me feet. It went to the shops, to school, everywhere. When I got into trouble for being naughty it was usually because that ball had gone over into the next-door neighbour's garden and damaged their flowers. I know it's hard to believe, but I did occasionally lose control. Mam used to have to give me a clip around the ear from time to time but it wasn't because I was playing up, it was because I was playing too much. She'd call me in at 7 o'clock and I would say, 'Just five more minutes, Mam.' She'd have to come out and drag me in.

If it wasn't football, it was 'kerby', standing on the pavement and throwing the ball against the opposite kerb, trying to get it to bounce back. If I got it spot on I'd sometimes header it or trap it on me chest. It all helped my close ball control.

At seven I was small but I was chubby. Every Sunday I used to go to Saltwell Park in Gateshead where there would always be a load of games on. I liked playing with the older boys and I could cope because I was quite sturdy. It was during those early days that I first learnt how to shield the ball and keep it away from the defenders. They were bigger and faster than me, but if they couldn't get the ball, there wasn't much they could do. That became a bit of a trademark when I got older and there are loads of photos of me doing it in this book.

'I'd only ever played with a tennis ball, knocking it against a wall in the playground or out in the street. When I was eventually given a proper ball, I found playing with it a doddle. That tennis ball probably helped shape me career.'

When I was about twelve me mam got a call from a TV programme called *Robson's Choice*. I don't know how they got my name, through the school perhaps, or the boys' club I was playing for at the time. Anyway, the show was what you would call reality TV now I suppose. It followed a bunch of young lads like me down at Ipswich Town, as Bobby Robson put us through our paces. We stayed in dormitories for a week and it was great. I was so excited being on television. I remember the first time I saw the cameras I gave one of me big cheeky-chappie grins and then slipped and went straight on my arse. I felt a right idiot.

We got to meet a lot of the players while we were there, people like Terry Butcher and Mick Mills. I remember talking to John Wark one day and asking him what it was like to score goals in big matches. He said it was the best feeling ever. He made it sound so great that I started laughing, I was so excited. I wanted to be like him and share that experience. I think he thought I was off me rocker.

I suppose this was me first trial for a professional club, but I didn't really think of it like that. All I cared about was being on the telly. Bobby Robson was great with all the kids, really kind, treating us as grown-ups and explaining how hard it was to become a professional footballer. I like to think he took a particular shine to me because he was a Geordie too. I definitely took a shine to him because he was the only one there who could understand me. But I obviously didn't stand out enough because I never heard anything more from Ipswich once the programme ended. Perhaps it was because of the Mars bars I was always eating... Who knows? I wasn't too bothered though. Ipswich was so far away from Newcastle it might as well have been on Mars. (Clever, eh?)

The boys' club I played for was called Redheugh. Me dad used to walk us there every night and once he had dropped us off he would slip away for a couple of pints and then come back to pick me up at nine. It meant I was getting home pretty late and sometimes I was tired at school. I have always been good at getting up in the morning, still am, and if I wasn't paying as much attention in the classroom as I should have been, it didn't bother me. All I cared about was football.

I won my first trophy at twelve years old, the Gateshead Schools penalty kick competition. I was buzzing afterwards. Penalties have played a big part in my football life. There must have been about 180 kids in the competition. There can't have been any German lads in the area at the time because I made it through to the final and scored twelve out of twelve to win. I kept the trophy under my pillow for weeks, I wouldn't let anyone else touch it. It meant that much to me.

A little while after *Robson's Choice,* I was offered a trial at Middlesbrough, which was much nearer to home than Ipswich. The day before I wasn't allowed to play for Redheugh in case I hurt myself and missed me chance. I went to watch the game and at some point the ball was blasted over a fence. I went to get it and when I jumped down a big lump of glass went straight through my shoe and into me foot. I was rushed to hospital and needed stitches so I missed the trial. I was gutted. Looking back now, it was a sign of things to come – missing out on playing, due to injury. Not that I knew that then.

'I kept the trophy under my pillow for weeks, I wouldn't let anyone else touch it. It meant that much to me.'

I got invited back shortly after for another go at Middlesbrough and I did really well. I remember sitting in the office of the bloke who ran the trials and noticing a brand new pair of trainers in the corner. They looked like they were about my size. I stared longingly at them for a moment and then told him I was definitely going to sign. He took the bait. Pointing towards the trainers, he said, 'I noticed you having a look. Do you like them?' I said I thought they were brilliant and he said I could have them. I was made up. I should have said I liked the table and chairs as well. Mam was looking for some new furniture for the house.

As it turned out, I didn't sign for Middlesbrough because I was still hoping that Newcastle would come knocking. But they were taking their time.

Next up was Southampton. They were doing the trials in Gateshead, so that was alright, but it was the only thing that was good about it. Even as a kid I thought the training was crap, not as good as we did at Redheugh. They were keen to sign us but I told me dad I didn't want to go, so that was that.

I eventually got a knock on the door from Newcastle United. I'd not long turned thirteen and I was over the moon. (That's what they say in football. I was learning fast.) Jimmy Nelson, who ran the youth academy, and Peter Kirtley, who was also involved in the club's youth development, spoke to Mam saying they wanted to sign me. Peter took me to watch some ice hockey and then we had some lunch and an ice cream. They were really looking after me and I kept thinking, this is brilliant, so I agreed to sign. I would have anyway though, even if Peter hadn't treated me so well. I loved the club. It was the only team I wanted to play for.

I went training twice a week, on a Tuesday and Thursday. We weren't paid, like, we were just schoolboys, but you were allowed to claim travel expenses. That was the bollocks. I used to get the bus there and then run home, but I'd say I had got a taxi and pocket the fiver expenses. Well, I didn't actually pocket it for very long. Whenever I arrived home Mam would be on the doorstep with her hand out. I had to give her the money. Fair enough, I suppose. I didn't mind. I've always been generous, me.

When I first signed as a schoolboy for the Toon, Billy McGarry was the manager but I never got to know him because he was out on his ear by the end of the summer and Arthur Cox was in.

Jimmy Nelson, from the youth academy, was the nicest guy you could meet, but Colin Suggett, who coached the youth team having finished his playing career at St James', was something else. If he saw some potential in someone he would come down on them like a tonne of bricks. He was always pushing me and if I did anything wrong he would give me extra training, making me run my bollocks off alone, after the normal training had finished.

'We weren't paid, like, we were just schoolboys,
but you were allowed to claim travel expenses.
That was the bollocks. I used to get the bus there
and then run home, but I'd say I had got a taxi
and pocket the fiver expenses.'

I can see now that he acted like that to toughen all the lads up, to help prepare them if they did make it. That was the right thing to do, of course, but at the time I just thought he was a right bastard.

Years later, when I eventually played my first game for Newcastle thought I was the business and I remember telling Colin to fuck off at training. He told all the other apprentices to go home and then he ran me until I was sick, before making me clean everything in the dressing room. As I was hard at it Arthur Cox came in and asked what had happened. When Colin told him, Arthur looked at me and I thought he was going to kill us. 'Right, it's my son's sixth birthday tomorrow. We're having a party here in the gym for him and his friends. I want the floor so spotless that they can eat their jelly off it.' I had to sweep and hoover and polish for hours.

Even though they were tough on me, I had loads of time for all the staff there. They taught me respect for my elders and for professional footballers. Another time, Arthur Cox asked me to make him a cup of coffee. I took it over with my hands round the top of the mug. I put it down on his desk only to receive a clip round the ear for me trouble. 'Don't put your horrid little chubby fingers near where I have to drink from.'

Later in my career, when I was at Spurs, we played away at Derby when Arthur was manager there. I got sent off in the match and after the final whistle I was in the dressing room, about to get a hard time from Terry Venables, when there was a knock at the door and one of the apprentices fearfully poked his head around. 'Sorry Boss. Arthur Cox wants to see Paul Gascoigne.' I went to Arthur's office, still with me kit on, and the moment I walked in he tore into me, so bad I started to cry. 'You've let yourself down, your family, me, your fans, your club, the country.' He went on and on, giving it plenty of slaps to me head to make sure I got the point. I learnt a lot from that, about what it means to be a footballer. It stuck with me, most of the time...

As a schoolboy I used to train sometimes with the full apprentices. It was a big jump as I was only about fifteen but I loved it. It pushed me beyond what I was used to at school, or even at Redheugh. By then some of me teachers had taken a real interest in my education – me football education, that is. They let me stay behind after class and play five-a-side with them. I wasn't exactly a model pupil so perhaps they had an extra motive. If I'd been a pain during the day and they hadn't been able to smack me arse, they used to get stuck right into me on the pitch. I didn't mind. It was another thing that helped toughen me up.

Not all the teachers saw my potential. Once in geography class everyone was concentrating hard on something totally fascinating that hadn't quite grabbed my attention, definitely not as much as practising my signature. I was writing 'Paul Gascoigne, Paul Gascoigne, Paul Gascoigne' over and over again, to get it just right. The teacher, Mr Hepworth, noticed my studious look and asked what I was doing.

'I'm practising my autograph, sir.' Everybody turned towards me and put down their pens.

'What do you mean?'

'I am going to be a professional footballer, sir.' He kicked off then, telling me that only one in a million make it. 'And you are not that one in a million, Gascoigne.'

'Yeah, alright sir.'

I carried on practising until he threw me out on me ear into the corridor. Years later, after the World Cup in Italy, about the first trip I made when we landed back in England was to my old school, to show the kids me shirt and all that. Everything was exactly the same, even Mr Hepworth teaching his geography class. I went up and tapped on his door. He looked up, saw me, smiled and gestured for me to come in. 'I know what you are going to say, Paul, and fair enough. I was wrong. You were that one in a million. Congratulations.' It was nice of him.

In the summer of 1982, the messiah arrived on Tyneside – Kevin Keegan signed for Newcastle.

I was Kevin's boot boy after he joined. Lucky him. He took a size seven and I took a size eight back then but when he asked me one day, 'Lad, what size boot do you wear?' I was so in awe of him I mumbled, 'Eh, an...an...eigh...seven.'

'Great. You can wear in this pair for me.'

They nearly killed me but I didn't care. I was wearing Kevin Keegan's boots! I was so excited that I decided to take them home, so I could show all me mates at school the next day. On the bus the following morning I was making a big thing of how I had the world's greatest player's boots, showing off and having a right laugh... Until I got off the bus and realised I was missing one.

I started to cry. I couldn't think what to do, so I tried to get on every bus in Gateshead to see if I could find it. Then I came up with a brilliant idea. I got them to put out an announcement over the tannoy at the big shopping centre: 'If anyone has found a single football boot today it is Kevin Keegan's. Can you please hand it in to the information desk.' It was bound to be turned in after that...

Next day I was so worried about what Keegan would say that I asked me dad to come to the ground with me to explain what had happened. Dad spoke to Kevin and said how sorry I was. I don't think he was too happy at the start but then he just laughed. 'It's alright. I've got loads anyway.' I never got to play with him at Newcastle – he'd gone by the time I made the first team – but I did line up alongside him a few years later in a charity match. Top man that Kevin Keegan. Still had small feet, mind.

CHAPTER 2

HARD CORE

NEWCASTLE:
MAY 1983 – JULY 1988

I signed as an apprentice with Newcastle on my sixteenth birthday.

It was a proper apprenticeship – hard – but I loved it. You had to look after the players' boots, make sure they were dry and polished, clean up the dressing room, all that. I got twenty-five quid a week and me mam was earning more, thirty-five a week, to feed and look after me. That was alright. It was payback time for everything she'd done for me when I was a kid. Obviously at sixteen I was no longer a kid, I was a man. That's what I thought anyway. Didn't act like it very often, mind.

I worked hard as an apprentice, but that didn't stop us mucking around and being cheeky. I remember pinching a tractor once that had been parked near the training pitch. I guess the groundsmen used it – I don't think there were any farmers in the Toon team. I managed to start it up, but I had no idea how to steer and jumped off just in time before it smashed into the wall of the changing rooms. I got a bollocking for that, and a fine.

Being an apprentice in those days was the best way to learn your trade. You were in amongst it all and could see and hear everything. Newcastle were playing Nottingham Forest one day and us lads were allowed to stand on the touchline, near to the away-team bench. At some point during the match Dave McCreery beat Johnny Metgod in the air. The Forest manager, Brian Clough of course, was not happy and didn't try to hide it. After an incredible string of swear words he turned to us apprentices and said, 'Which one of you young men is a midfield player?' They all pointed at me. 'Do you bottle it like that big lump out there?' 'No, sir,' I said, terrified of the great man. 'Good lad. I'll keep my eye on you to make sure that's true.'

'It was a proper apprenticeship – hard – but I loved it. You had to look after the players' boots, make sure they were dry and polished, clean up the dressing room, all that.'

Cloughie's and my paths didn't cross that often during my career but I will never forget one match when I was at Spurs. We were at home against Forest and I made a run, beat a couple of defenders, but just failed to keep the ball in. The ref blew for a goal kick and I started to walk back up the pitch. Just then, I heard someone shouting, 'Gascoigne, Gascoigne, get back to your team.' It didn't sound like my manager, Terry Venables, so I looked up. It was Cloughie. It took me straight back to that time as an apprentice. 'Okay, sorry, Gaffer,' I shouted and ran back to the middle of our half, glancing at Terry as I passed. He just smiled and shrugged his shoulders.

There were all sorts of characters around the club at that time. I remember early on, after I'd signed as an apprentice, the manager Arthur Cox had pinned the team sheet up on the wall and me and the other lads were looking at it to see who was playing. I was running my finger down the names when out of nowhere I got a massive clip around me ear. It was the boss. It was so hard I felt like crying. (Not like me, I know.) 'You don't touch that until you're on it.' I didn't, not for another eighteen months.

'Arthur Cox had pinned the team sheet up on the wall and me and the other lads were looking at it to see who was playing. I was running my finger down the names when out of nowhere I got a massive clip around me ear.'

The great Jackie Milburn was around the ground a lot. He had signed for the club during the war and was a legend on Tyneside. He used to give the vote for player of the month and he would say to me, 'Score one today, lad, and you've got it.' It gave me such a buzz – someone like that taking an interest in me. And I must have listened because I earned a good collection of those silver plates.

Another legendary ex-player who encouraged me was Joe Harvey. He played around the same time as Jackie Milburn and went on to manage the Toon for about a hundred years. He was a touch more forthright than Wor Jackie. 'Listen, Gascoigne, you change the way you play today and I'll fucking have you. Be artistic, take them all on. Fuck them.' That was his team talk to me when I was about to run out. I loved it.

BIG JACK

Arthur Cox resigned and Jack Charlton took over from him in the summer of 1984, not long after I turned seventeen. Despite the surprise change of manager and the retirement of Keegan, it was a good time at St James' Park. The first team had just won promotion to the First Division and I'd broken into the youth team. I thought I'd done pretty well, for about a day.

Jack Charlton called me in to see him not long after he arrived. 'You're a good player Gascoigne.'

'Yeah, aye,' I said, pleased with meself.

'How long is your contract for?'

'Two years,' I replied, all cocky.

'Wrong. You've got two weeks, you fat bastard. If you don't train, i'll have you for breakfast and then spit you out.'

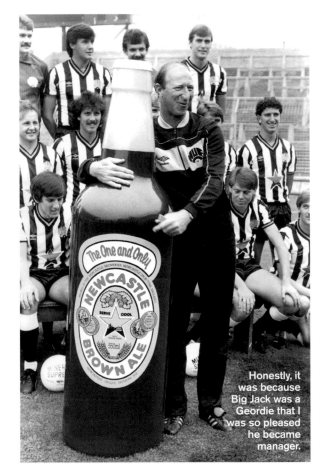

Honestly, it was because Big Jack was a Geordie that I was so pleased he became manager.

I thought me days were numbered, but Jack made me stick to a new training regime. He got the runner, Brendan Foster, involved to help. I had to run wearing a plastic bin bag to work up a real sweat and was put on a diet of steaks and salad and things like that. He really pushed me because he believed in me. But it was murder. I used to get so knackered that I would fall asleep on the train home and end up in all sorts of places. I'll never forget Jack saying to me after those two weeks, 'Listen son, the time to worry is when I stop bollocking you. One day you'll appreciate this.' He was right. I do.

THIS IS BRILLIANT

All the hard work paid off. Big Jack didn't spit me out. In fact, he gave me my first team debut. I had made it on to the bench once before, for a game against Sunderland, but hadn't got on the pitch. For the next match, against QPR on 13 April 1985, I was sitting next to the gaffer and kept asking him questions like, 'Why have you got him?' pointing to our physio, who was about seventy. 'He's very old.' 'For his cigarettes. Now shut it.' I didn't stop talking though and eventually Big Jack had had enough.

'Get yourself on. I'll give you five minutes.'

I was excited and shitting myself at the same time. I got the ball almost immediately, about thirty yards from their goal. I froze – couldn't think what to do. So I turned round and booted it back to our keeper. The Gallowgate End must have thought they had a real superstar on their hands.

Before the game me dad had said to me, 'If you get on, get buckled right in!' I thought, fair enough, but I can still be nice to someone. Robbie James was the QPR captain and as I ran past him I said, 'This is brilliant, isn't it?' I remember him saying 'Fuck off,' and a moment later I got stretchered off the pitch. Apparently he'd elbowed me in the throat. Not that I knew anything about it at the time – I was out for the count. I had barely been on for sixty seconds! I eventually came round and played the last two minutes.

So my debut lasted a grand total of three minutes, but I didn't care. The buzz was amazing. I was a Newcastle United player. When the final whistle went, and we'd won 1–0, the Gallowgate End erupted. It was everything I'd ever dreamed it would be and I wanted more.

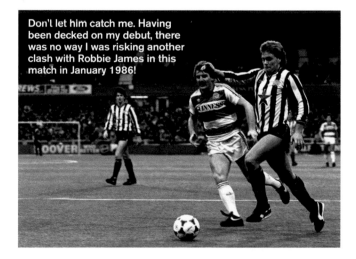

Don't let him catch me. Having been decked on my debut, there was no way I was risking another clash with Robbie James in this match in January 1986!

JOYS OF YOUTH

Almost immediately after the QPR game it was back to business as normal for me, not just in training but playing-wise as well. I was still only seventeen and a member of the Newcastle youth team, captain in fact, and we'd had a great run that year in the FA Youth Cup, making the final against Watford. We had an unbelievable squad and were red-hot favourites but Watford held us nil-all at St James'. In the second leg, though, on 10 May 1985, we mullered them. I scored twice and so did Joe Allon, to win 4–1. They had no chance really, when you look at the team we had then, with the likes of Jeff Wrightson, Ian Bogie and Paul Stephenson. Almost all of the team made at least a handful of appearances for the Newcastle senior team. More than twenty-five years later I can still remember all their names and I'm going to prove it to you. They were great lads.

Standing, left to right: Paul Stephenson, Tony Hayton, Brian Kilford, Peter Harbach, Kevin Scott, Gary Kelly (goalie), Ian Bogie, Brian Tinnion, Tony Nesbit, Jeff Wrightson (just in picture), Stephen Forster. In the front that's me and Joe Allon.

Right after the final, Big Jack asked me whether I wanted to play the next day in the first team at Norwich. I froze and said no, I want to go back with the guys. Even though I had already tasted senior action, inside I was still worried that it could all disappear. I knew I was tired and I didn't want to blow it. I think Jack understood. He certainly didn't hold it against me because he let me know there and then that he wanted me to sign as a professional.

There was no negotiation and barely any discussion. I said yes, and he told me what I would be getting paid – £120 a week and £120 for each game I played, on a four-year contract. I thought that was brilliant. Mind you, I would have probably signed for nothing if he had said that was the deal. I was shit scared of him, although I thought he was awesome at the same time.

SEASONED PRO

I couldn't wait for the new season, 1985/86, to begin. I wanted the summer to rush past so I could try and establish myself in the first team. I hated the holidays. Six weeks without playing football – what was that all about? After my first year as an apprentice, on me seventeenth birthday at the end of May 1984, I had cried me eyes out when the season came to an end. I was heartbroken, and although it was daft, I thought that was it for me and the club wouldn't want me back. I felt the same way in the summer of 1985. Anything could happen that might put an end to my dreams.

I got through it though, and we started pre-season in August. Newcastle had ended the previous campaign in fourteenth place and the fans were restless, especially after Chris Waddle left for Spurs in July. We were playing Sheffield

United in a friendly and I was sitting on the bench next to Big Jack when a chant of 'Charlton out! Charlton out!' began to ring around the stadium. Jack turned to me and said, 'I don't need this, Gaz. Good luck, son, in your career.' And that was it. He was gone. He stood up from the bench and went home. On the Sunday he went fishing, and on the Monday he resigned.

Willie McFaul took over and even with all the changes, I was really excited, especially when he picked me for my first start, in the opening game of the season, away to Southampton. What a buzz that was. As you can see in the photo on the previous page, I made sure to strike a few poses and oil me legs up so I looked the business. I felt properly part of the team, and even started yelling at the other players, telling them where to go and who to mark. Those debut nerves were long gone.

It was a weird time, the start of that season. One moment I'd be playing in front of the Gallowgate against Liverpool, taking on Kenny Dalglish, and the next I'd be on the bus home with the fans. I think it was after that Liverpool match, or perhaps the next one against Coventry, that I was first recognised. 'You were playing today, weren't you, son? Well done. You did well.' That gave me an unbelievable feeling.

Kenny was one of my heroes and when they got a corner one time I deliberately ran over to where he was standing, by the near post, just so I could touch him. It was ridiculous but I couldn't help it. 'Hiya Kenny,' I said to him. He wasn't amused. 'Piss off.' Fair enough.

One player who was brought in that autumn was Billy Whitehurst. He was massive. In training we used to work in pairs. Peter Beardsley would be up against Glenn Roeder and I would get Whitehurst. I don't know why, perhaps I'd done something to piss off the gaffer.

More than likely. Anyway, the idea was that he had the ball and I had to try and nick it off him. We worked on this a lot and one day I robbed him and slipped it through his legs. He was no gentle giant. 'If you do that one more time I will punch you in the fucking jaw.' Oof, no thank you, I thought, but a few moments later one of the other lads pinged the ball to me. It hit my shin and nutmegged Billy perfectly. Boom.

He put me on my arse. Bugger this, I thought, and ran off the pitch. I didn't go back for three days.

Top flight football was still populated by proper hard men back then. I had already had a taste of that with Robbie James and away in the League Cup at Oxford I received a full helping. The manager was giving his team talk before the match, and he turned to Peter Beardsley, 'You two, be careful. Look after each other. You've got Briggs and Shotton – they don't take prisoners.' Peter and I laughed nervously. Inside I was bricking it.

Gary Briggs and Malcolm Shotton were hard, tough defenders. From kick off, whenever they went into a challenge you could actually hear heads clattering. At one stage early on Peter was caught in a challenge and as he lay on the ground I watched as Shotton, still on top of him, whacked Peter on the chin. He was alright though, he's a brave lad and just got up and shrugged it off. I didn't fancy the game much after that.

Two minutes later it was my turn. Bang, I cracked my nose on a defender's elbow. I said to Beardsley, 'Peter, I think I've broken me nose,' and he looked at me and started to laugh. So did Glenn Roeder. I stayed on but there was only fifteen minutes gone. Bloody hell, I thought, what more can happen?

I took me chance when it came. Willie McFaul had obviously seen the clash and shouted across at me, 'You okay? Any double vision?', 'Yeah, Gaffer, I can't see a thing.' He pulled me off and I ran straight into the dressing room to look at me nose. It was all over my face! It hardly needs saying I burst into tears.

You can see how my broken nose affected me good looks here at Anfield a few weeks after it happened.

Under-soil heating? We didn't even bother with long sleeves. That's us Geordies for you.

The next morning I was still upset and had to go to hospital. Peter and Glenn picked us up and they still couldn't stop laughing. I had to get an operation to fix it – the first of many in my football career. The swelling was there for ages.

It wasn't just the players who were harder back then. It was the conditions as well. I can't see too many of the Premiership superstars of today being happy to slide around in the snow like we had to in this match against Forest in February 1986. Mind you, it was a good job it was so cold. Forget Shotton and Briggs, even Robbie James, the hardest challenge I ever had in my career came in this match. From that well-known man of granite, Nigel Clough. Honestly, the way he timed it, he leathered me. My whole body shuddered. If I hadn't been so numb I think I'd still be in pain.

Until I let the lads down by hugging Peter Beardsley for warmth.

BOY ABOUT TOWN

During that first year loads happened for us. I was getting all kinds of sponsorship – Puma, Adidas – it was brilliant. I even got an agent, and one of the deals he got me was with a local garage. I got to drive around in this smart black Rover with me name down the side and on the bonnet. The garage had their name on it as well, which was fine, but they included their phone number. Not so clever.

I thought that Rover was the bollocks, until I began to get all these phone calls from the garage: 'Paul, is the car okay?' 'Yeah, fine.' 'Paul, you have passed your test, right?' 'Yeah, of course I have.' I ignored them to start with but after a month of this I was a bit pissed off. It was as though the garage didn't really want me to have the car. What I didn't know was that the fans had been ringing up and saying things like. 'Oh I can't believe it. I've just seen Gazza in town, in his car. It's a lovely motor but he's just smashed it.' Or, 'He's just tried to run us over. And I'm with the kids.' Or, 'I've just seen him driving up a one-way street the wrong way.' It was all joking but it did become a bit of a nightmare so I gave the car back eventually. It's tough being a celebrity...

VINNIE

lough Lane, 6 February 1988. In the dressing room before the match Willie McFaul was giving his instructions. 'Right, Beardsley, you are up against the centre half. He's tough so be careful, try to take him on the inside. Roeder, you are up against the centre forward. He's fast.' He went through the whole team like that and then came to me. 'Paul, good luck.' Our skipper, Glenn Roeder, started laughing. 'Be careful out there, Paul. This Vinnie Jones character, he's supposed to be off his head.'

As we were walking up the tunnel I spotted Vinnie instantly. It was hard not to. Even then you didn't get too many skinhead hod carriers in the First Division. I had never heard of him before so I looked over and said, 'Hiya.' All friendly like. He turned to me and said,

'Fucking me and you, fat boy. Me and you.' If there was any doubt in my mind that I was in trouble, it had gone before kick off. During the warm-up Vinnie kept coming over to our side of the pitch to make sure I'd got his point. 'Me and you, fat boy. Me and you. I can't play, I know that, but neither will you today.'

I began to panic a bit which only got worse three seconds after the ref blew his whistle. Wimbledon kicked off and played the ball back to the midfield, but Vinnie totally ignored it and ran up to me. 'But you've got the ball!' I shouted. 'I don't want the fucking ball. I want you.'

He was all over me from that moment, following us everywhere, rattling into us whenever he could. At one point I knocked the ball through his legs and I thought he was going to smash us.

Early on they got a corner and I was standing there thinking, for fuck's sake, I've got ninety minutes of this, when suddenly he was right in front of me, sneering. 'Ya! Fat boy!' I nearly jumped out of me skin. 'I forgot to tell you. I take the corners. I won't be long. Make sure you are here when I get back.' So I stood like an idiot on the pitch waiting for him.

The fans could hear all this and were killing themselves. Next they got a throw in. 'Fat boy, I also take the throw ins. Don't move.' 'I've got it. Don't worry. I won't go far.' Then I sort of came to my senses and thought what the hell am I doing? I decided to try and get my own back, to start pushing him around, marking him close. Bad mistake.

I got too tight, way too tight. That's when he squeezed me knackers. I looked to the linesman and squealed but no one had seen anything. Vinnie didn't say a word. He didn't need to. I was petrified enough.

For the record, it ended a hard-earned nil-all. I like to think our point was thanks to me keeping their danger man occupied. After the game Vinnie came up and hugged me. I thought that was class. 'I am sorry about that, Gazza, I had to do it. I couldn't let you make a mug of me on the pitch.' In the dressing room afterwards I was sent a rose from a girl in the crowd and I asked one of the apprentices to give it to Vinnie. 'Tell him it's from Gazza with love.' He sent a toilet brush back.

When I moved down to London with Spurs, Vinnie was one of the first people to come and meet me at my hotel. I thought it was going to be round two but he just said, 'I've come to show you around.' That was really nice of him and we became mates. I even went to stay with him for a few days and he took me pigeon shooting. It was almost the last thing he did. I nearly shot him. What a loss to Hollywood that would have been. I was carrying me shotgun and Vinnie said, 'Gaz, always break the stock when you're not shooting.' 'That's okay, Vinnie,' I said, waving it around. 'It's not loaded.' Wrong. It went off and missed him by about a yard. All I could think of was what the headlines would have been the next day. 'Gazza gets his own back.' Top man, Vinnie. Still is.

'I decided to try and get my own back,
to start pushing him around, marking
him close. Bad mistake.'

FAREWELL TOON

By the time Vinnie nearly lost me my family allowance I was well into my third full year as a first team regular and I was fairly pleased with how things had gone for me personally. In spite of the odd injury I was approaching one hundred appearances in all competitions and would go on to score a total of twenty-five goals. Not bad for a stocky midfielder, and I was sure I would get better. But I wasn't convinced the club matched me ambitions. Peter Beardsley had already buggered off to Liverpool and even though there were some new faces in the changing room, there wasn't much buzz about the place. By then I'd played a few times for England Under-21s and I'd loved it. But what I really wanted was a shot at the senior side and I began to think that a fresh start might be me only chance. Trouble was, Newcastle didn't want to sell us.

I took matters into me own hands. I got me mate Jimmy Gardner involved, naturally. I asked him to go to the newspapers and pretend he was on the staff at West Ham (well he was so sporty looking), and say that they were coming in with a million quid for me. I picked West Ham because they looked a quality club with passionate fans, just like Newcastle.

Strangely, my final appearance for Newcastle was against West Ham, on 7 May 1988. I was sad but I couldn't let on as nothing had been settled yet with a move. At the end of the match I didn't make a big thing of going up to the Gallowgate. It was the last game of the season and we were celebrating a respectable eighth-place finish so all the players gave the supporters a big wave to say thanks. I was also saying something extra. Thanks and goodbye. I knew I would never play in front of them again as a Newcastle player. It was time to move on but not to the East End as it turned out. I was on me way to North London...eventually.

CHAPTER 3

LION CUB

ENGLAND:
JUNE 1987 – JUNE 1990

I was never selected for the England Schoolboys team. Not that I am annoyed about that or anything, but I'll tell you what happened. The first trial I was invited to, the guy who ran it gave me only ten minutes on the pitch. I never had the chance to do anything. Then I was invited for a second, which consisted of three fifteen-minute sessions. He told me I'd get a chance in the third one and I realised I'd better do something a bit special. Like score a hat trick. Which I did. And did I hear another word from them? Did I fuck. I think the reason was that he had other boys there from his own school and he picked them above me. Their family fitted where mine didn't. I never forgave the bloke for that. But as I say, I am not annoyed about it or anything...

I was nineteen when Willie McFaul called me into his office at Newcastle United. 'Listen Paul, I've got some bad news for you. You've missed out on the England Under-19 squad. I'm sorry.' I know it sounds daft, me being nineteen already, but I really was eligible at the time. Honestly. When he said it I was so disappointed. It was the Schoolboys all over again. 'Are you sure, Boss?' 'Yes, I'm afraid so. But you are going to be in the Under-21s!' He was a right card, Mr McFaul.

Dave Sexton was the Under-21s manager at the time and he was hard-core. In team talks he never wrote on a board to show the formation and tactics. Instead he used the chairs in the dressing room. He would move them around and explain who had to go here and who had to go there. What a laugh, it was brilliant. And it all made perfect sense. He was a great manager and I had a huge amount of respect for him. He used to say to me, 'Paul, if you keep at it like you are, keep playing the way you do, you'll make the first team in no time.' I appreciated that.

Pulling on that England shirt for the first time was an unbelievable feeling, and to top a brilliant day off nicely, I scored. It was from a free kick against Morocco in the Toulon International Tournament in France on 7 June 1987. Just before the ref blew the whistle to take the kick I noticed the keeper coming off his line a bit to peer round the wall to see where I was aiming. As the ref put the whistle to his lips I gestured to one of our lads to move to the back post. As he did, the keeper was distracted and I whacked it inside the near post. To be fair he got his hand to it but he shouldn't have bothered. It was always going into the back of the net. What a feeling! Me dad was behind the goal with his mates which made it even better. One England game, one goal. Over the course of almost fifteen months I won thirteen Under-21 caps, scored five goals and played with some top-class lads.

This is before the game against West Germany on 8 September 1987. In this line-up alone Tony Dorigo, David Rocastle, Paul Davis, Tony Cottee, Des Walker and Nigel Clough (and me) all made it through to full internationals. If you are thinking Paul Davis, top row, third from left, looks a bit like our granddad, that's because you were allowed one over-age player. Paul was brilliant and playing alongside him in the Under-21s was a great opportunity. When I first joined the squad I told him he looked a lot older than the rest of us. 'That's because I am twenty-three, Gazza.' I nodded intelligently. 'Ah, that's why you are so good – you're an old geezer.'

I had been dropped before this game against Yugoslavia in November 1987 which was a bit of a shock and probably just what I needed. When I regained my place in the squad I was determined not to let Dave Sexton down and I don't think I did, scoring twice in our 5–1 victory.

In February 1988 we played Scotland. There was a big build-up before the match – who was the best up-and-coming player in Britain, me or Rangers' Ian Durrant? No contest. Durranty pissed all over me. He was flying that day. He got Man of the Match and was absolutely brilliant. You could tell he was an outstanding footballer with an incredible future. Then eight months

later he suffered a terrible knee injury in a game against Aberdeen. It was just horrible and I think it is fair to say he never fully recovered to realise the astonishing potential he'd showed against us. I played with Ian when I went to Rangers years later, but not often. We had similar games which made it difficult for the gaffer, Walter Smith, to accommodate us both. I tended to get the nod which can't have been easy for Ian but you would never have known it. Throughout my three years at Rangers, Durranty was quality in every sense. A great lad.

BOBBY ROBSON CALLS

n September 1988 I failed to make the Under-21s again, because Bobby Robson had given me a call-up to the full squad. God, I was buzzing. There were seven debutants for the game against Denmark. Here's a photograph of us all with the manager – Alan Smith, Michael Thomas, Des Walker, David Rocastle, Paul Davis, Mel Sterland and me.

I've also included a close-in photo on the next page with me and Sir Bobby (as he later became) just because I love it. It says everything about the man, the way he is smiling with his arm around me. He was like a second dad – always looking after me and looking out for me, right up to the end. A few days before he passed away in 2009 he was watching a charity game that I was playing in, against Germany. He could hardly recognise me, but he knew my voice. His son told me later that when they were on their way home Sir Bobby turned to him and asked, 'Son, how did that Gascoigne play today?' I had a lump in my throat when I heard that. I loved the man.

I didn't really know Sir Bobby, though, when I was called up for the full England squad. I'd met him when I had been down in Ipswich for that TV programme, *Robson's Choice* and again a couple of times, briefly, when he came in to the Under-21s dressing room after a match to say hello. He obviously remembered us though because he said on one occasion, 'Well played today, son. You did well. But are you still eating those Mars bars?' That made me giggle.

I'd moved to Spurs by then and it was Terry Venables who told me I'd been selected for the squad when we were at training at Spurs. I couldn't quite believe it. The England team! Me, the boy from Dunston! I know people say this all the time, but it really was a dream come true. Terry also explained that when I turned up at the England training camp I had to make sure to bring a white shirt, to attend some function or other. On arrival, Bobby Robson asked me whether I'd remembered, so I said, 'Yeah Boss, I've brought one white shirt. I'll leave the other one to you.' He liked that.

I came on with about five minutes to go in the match against Denmark. I didn't care that it was only for such a short time. It felt like hours and I had enough touches of the ball to feel like I'd contributed. Dreams really do come true sometimes.

'I've brought one white shirt. I'll leave the other one to you.'

DAFT AS A BRUSH

I got another run out in a friendly against Saudi Arabia a couple of months later and then in my first proper competitive match for England, a World Cup qualifier against Albania at Wembley, I scored – this is it here. There can be no better feeling in the world, okay in football, than scoring for your country – the pride, the excitement, the honour – amazing.

I remember the ball coming to me on the right. One of their defenders put in a challenge but I brushed him off and suddenly there was an opening in front of me. I decided to give it a crack with me left and I caught it lovely. Right in the back of the net. The roar was deafening.

To be honest, I didn't know what to do next. How do you celebrate scoring for England? I had no routine worked out. Then Chris Waddle and Peter Beardsley came over, high-fiving and both so pleased for me. Three Geordies together – it was brilliant. Anyone who wants to play football wants to score for their country and I was no different. All I could think about was that me dad would be watching the match on TV with his mates in the working men's club at home. That made me smile.

The only problem with the Albania game was that I hadn't exactly done what I'd been told. Bobby Robson had sent me on with about twenty-five minutes to go with precise instructions to stay on the right. I thought he said, 'You can stray around alright.' Well, not really. I was just too excited to stick to one position. I wanted as many touches of the ball as possible to show what I could do. I reckon a headless chicken would have been more disciplined. This was the first time Sir Bobby called me 'daft as a brush' and I couldn't blame him.

After the game he spoke to the press. 'Every time we are going to play him we need two balls. One for him and one for the team. At one time I thought he was going to play in the front row of F stand because he played all over the pitch except in the position I told him to play in.' Oops. But at least I scored. He was happy with that.

Mmm, let me think... How many balls will we need if Gascoigne plays?

BLOODY HELL

I made my first England start against Chile at Wembley in the Rous Cup and then came on as a sub in the following match against Scotland, but after that I didn't appear in the all-important World Cup qualifier against Poland or the next friendly, against Denmark. I was beginning to worry that my Albanian antics had actually put Sir Bobby off me for the big matches, especially as England were very solid in the midfield.

Neil Webb and Bryan Robson were an inseparable pairing and played consistently well together. If I was going to make the 1990 World Cup squad, and that was all I was thinking about – get in the squad, get in the squad, get in the squad – I began to contemplate changing position. A five-foot-ten-inch Geordie lad taking over from Shilts in goal? It seemed unlikely.

That's why I was so chuffed when Sir Bobby called me up for the crucial qualifier against Sweden in Stockholm. I didn't expect to get on, but then Neil Webb did his Achilles with about twenty-five minutes to go. This is the injury that ultimately put paid to his career. It was horrible for him, but no one then knew the extent of the problem. All I knew was that I was about to get my chance.

Guess which one came on late in the match?

We battled hard for a scoreless draw and a vital point. Captain Terry Butcher gave it everything he had, literally blood, sweat and tears (well, probably not the last one knowing Terry). I walked off the pitch with him at the end, me all clean and fresh looking, him like something out of a Hammer Horror film. He was taken straight to the treatment room where Sir Bobby went in to see how he was doing.

All of a sudden the door bursts open and Robson marches out shouting, 'Where is he? Where is he?' I was wondering which poor bugger he was looking for. Then he spots me, 'There you are. Come here,' and leads me into the room where Butcher is lying on a table getting stitched up. 'Look at him, Gascoigne. Pouring with blood and he still carries on. That's what it means to play for England.' I thought, he's right – that is what it means to play for your country. You give all you've got. Every time.

BOOKING A HOLIDAY

England qualified for the 1990 World Cup with a nil-all against Poland in October 1989, sadly without me, but I was given my chance to prove what I was made of in a friendly against Czechoslovakia the following April. I'd had a run out against Brazil in March but I knew this was the do or die game. Play well and I had a chance of making it to Italia '90, screw up and I faced another miserable summer waiting for the season to begin.

I played a blinder. Set up three and scored one. That's what I say anyway. Bobby Robson disagreed. He said I'd only set up two because taking a corner didn't count if the ball was flicked on before it was put in. There were times when he clearly didn't understand football.

For my goal, in the last minute, which you can see here, Tony Dorigo passed it to me and I went straight at the defence forcing them to make a decision, to go for the tackle or try and steer me away from goal. The minute I saw the defender commit one way, I knew I had him. I cut inside and hit a left-footer. I intended to just smash it towards goal but I caught it even better than I had intended and it ended up in the top corner. Later, I watched the highlights on TV and as the ball hit the back of the net the camera cut to Bobby Robson as he turned to Don Howe saying, 'That's fantastic.'

One of the things about Bobby Robson, which is different from other England managers apart from Terry Venables, was that if you played well for England, regardless of how you are doing for your club, you kept your place in the national team. Sir Bobby believed in keeping a settled side and so when I saw what he said on TV I knew I'd made it into the squad. All I need to wait for now, I thought, is the call asking me to come in to get me suit measured. When I was told I had made the squad, I was flying, like an over-excited kid with a lollipop.

I was off on me holidays.

CHAPTER 4

LONDON CALLING

SPURS:
JULY 1988 – MAY 1992

At Newcastle, prior to my England call-up, I began to hear stories of legitimate interest in signing me after stoking the fire with my West Ham tale. Apparently Manchester United and Liverpool were both in the hunt, as were Celtic, although nothing ever came of that. It would be years before I moved to Glasgow, to the other side of the city.

I fancied the idea of playing for Liverpool a lot. Kenny Dalglish was the manager and I spoke to him about a possible move to Anfield but the timing wasn't right for them. They had just re-signed Ian Rush from Juventus and didn't have the cash available to make another big purchase. Newcastle were looking for 2.2 million quid for me – a fortune back then. Nowadays it wouldn't even pay for Andy Carroll's shampoo bill. Kenny asked me to hang on a year and then they would sign us, when they had raised the money, but that wasn't going to work for me. I'd already made me mind up to go.

I was torn between Spurs and Man U. The thought of playing alongside Bryan Robson was a big draw. And of course, there was Fergie himself. He hadn't yet taken United to the heights he would, but you could tell there was something special going on there. But that was part of the problem. The Newcastle supporters weren't exactly thrilled that I was leaving anyway, and if I went to Man U, strengthening their squad, I don't think they would have ever forgiven us.

Then there was Spurs. Glenn Roeder spoke to me about them, saying what a good team they were and how I would fit in there. I respected Glenn so his opinion mattered. And of course me mate Chris Waddle was there. I loved playing with him and not only that, he could act as a translator for me. The Spurs manager, Terry Venables, was also a factor. I knew he was top quality from his days at Barcelona but I didn't know him at all. I had only met Terry briefly after we had beaten them 2–0 back in January. I had played a bit of a blinder, mullering Terry Fenwick in the middle and scoring both goals. Apparently this was the game that persuaded Spurs to buy us. I was sponsored by Hummel to wear their boots and they were also the Spurs sponsors. After the match Terry came up to me and said, 'Well the only good thing I can say about today is that at least you are wearing the right boots.' That made me laugh.

So I was confused about where to move to and I admit I didn't handle it very well. At one stage I had pretty much made up me mind that it was going to be United. I had even arranged to have a look round and discuss it all. Then on the way I got a call on me massive mobile phone. It was Spurs' chairman Irving Scholar offering to buy a house for me mam and dad. 'Oh, right. Thanks Mr Scholar. I'll get back to you.' I really didn't know what to do so I decided not to go to Old Trafford that day. I needed time to think.

Fergie then gave us a call. He was about to go on holiday and he wanted to know what was happening. I did something a bit stupid, I panicked a bit. I don't like saying no to people, so I told him that he should go off and have a nice time and that I was definitely signing for United. 'Good lad,' he said. 'You've made the right decision.'

Only I hadn't made any decision. Not really. I went down to London to talk to Terry and Irving Scholar. I was very impressed by both

It was my style and sophistication that persuaded Spurs to sign me.

of them, and the set-up there. Terry said that if I came to Spurs he would guarantee that within ten games I'd get an England call-up. That was tempting, but I was also thinking that if I paired up with Robson at Man United, that could be a great England double act, so they both sort of cancelled each other out. Then they started piling on the extras, on top of the house. 'We'll get your sister a sunbed.'

'Right-o. Thanks very much.'

'And all the fishing gear you want. Plus a BMW for your dad.' That's what swung it eventually. I wasn't bothered about the wages they were offering, or even the house, it was more that me dad would love a new car.

Fergie wasn't too happy. Can't say I blame him. He wrote to me, saying how he couldn't believe what I had done and how stupid I had been to turn down the biggest club in the world. It took about seven years before I got on the right side of him again, but we are friendly now.

MEMORY LANE

I think I played the best football of me career at Tottenham. I loved it there and had a brilliant time, with a great bunch of lads. There were so many unbelievable moments that it has been a tough job picking just a few here for the book. I know I've missed some crackers out, but there just wasn't space. So here's a selection of the good...and the bad, of me time at White Hart Lane.

MARS ATTACK

I guess it was inevitable that I would make my competitive debut for Spurs against Newcastle. I think the Geordie faithful were pleased I hadn't gone across to Manchester but they were still pretty miffed that I had left and weren't shy in demonstrating it. Just as I was about to take a corner someone threw a frozen Mars bar at us. Cheeky bastards. It was funny, mind.

KNOCKING THEIR SOCKS OFF

One of my favourite goals of all time was my first for Spurs, even though we lost the match 3–2 to Arsenal. Chris Waddle was charging forward with the ball and I was on the edge of the box, marked by Paul Davis. There was space on the right and I could tell that Chris had seen it. Just as he slid the pass through and I made my move, Paul's boot caught the back of mine and flipped it off. I carried on the run and tried to knock the ball with

me sock under John Lukic. He saved it but I managed to slot home the rebound. With me sock again. I made sure to take my time walking back up the pitch so all the Arsenal lads could see I'd only needed one boot to score against them. They don't look too impressed.

GOAL MACHINE

Spurs signed Gary Lineker after I joined the club. I remember asking Terry Venables what he was like, and he said Lineker was incredible – one of the best strikers in the world. It didn't look that way after six matches when he had failed to find the net. I began to wonder what all the fuss was about. I mentioned this to Terry. 'I thought you said he was a bit special.'

'Just give him time. Once he gets going, that'll be it.'

He wasn't wrong and I was embarrassed that I had questioned him. Lineker opened his account in the very next match and went on to be the top scorer in the league. He really was a goal machine. Phenomenal. Along with Ally McCoist I'd say he was the best striker I ever played with. That's why I've included these photos – of me scoring one of me four against Hartlepool in the League Cup in 1990 – just to remind meself that I got a few too.

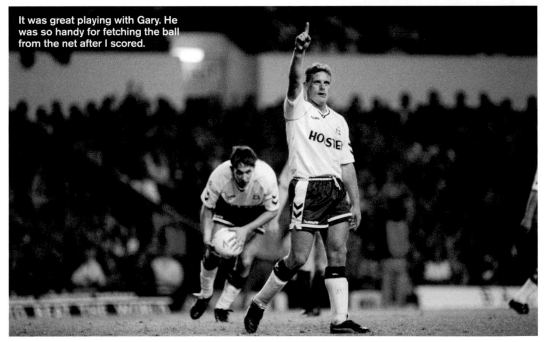

It was great playing with Gary. He was so handy for fetching the ball from the net after I scored.

Joking aside, it was great playing with Lineker. I know it's been said before, but he really was the perfect professional. We got on well and developed a brilliant partnership on the pitch. We had a secret sign we used when we were playing together, which told me whether Gary was going to spin off his defender, in which case I would know exactly where to play the ball, or stay with his back to goal, ready for a one-two. I guess we were lucky no one ever spotted what we were up to. We'd have been screwed if they had.

TRICK OF THE TRADE

Scoring a hat trick is always nice. Scoring one against the best keeper in the world? Priceless. It was in a match against Derby in September 1990. I didn't rib Shilton about it at the time, though, he was too much of an old-school professional to take the piss out of. But years later? Yeah, of course I did.

For the first goal I remember the ball came across the box and I hit it with me left foot, but I scuffed it a bit and it's gone under Shilts and into the back of the net.

The second one was a free kick on the edge of the box, on the right. Shilts had the wall set up lovely but he was standing a little too much to his right, my left. I caught it unbelievably. To be fair, no keeper would have saved it, but he tried hard, diving sort of funny – forward rather than on his side – and he ended up in the back of the net. After the ball that is.

The third was also a free kick, miles out. About forty yards. Shilts was organising his wall, standing with his hand on the post, lining it up just right, and I thought, fuck it, I'm going to give this a crack. 'Ref, can I take a quick one?' He nodded and I leathered it before poor Shilts really knew what was going on. He tried to scramble across but all he could do was watch it fly in. I remember him

throwing his hands up in the air afterwards and shaking his head as if to say, 'What the hell was that?' Lovely.

That hat trick was especially nice because it gave a V-sign to the press who around then were saying that after the World Cup I was getting involved in too much activity off the pitch. I never really understood why they thought that...

FA CUP – THE ROAD TO WEMBLEY

T he 1991 FA Cup run sort of sums up everything about me time at Spurs so I've decided to go through every round. This time holds happy memories for me. Mostly. Before then I had never had much luck in the cup, but there was something in the air that year. It was special, maybe because it was '91 and Spurs had picked up the trophy in 1901, 1921, 1961, and 1981. Perhaps it was destiny. Or just me being brilliant.

BLACKPOOL – 5 JANUARY 1991

Our first match was away to Blackpool and it was tough. The wind was fierce, whipping off the sea and making everything difficult. We got a free kick in the second half, on the right, near the halfway line. I decided to bang it in as hard as I could, to get it through the wind, and get it into the area where I knew Paul Stewart would be. It was something we had worked on in training and it was good seeing it come off when he got his head on it for the only goal of the game, against his old club.

Only one word for it: scintillating.

OXFORD – 26 JANUARY 1991

This was an important game for Spurs. There were a load of rumours flying around, about how we were in financial bother and needed someone to buy us out. So a cup run was essential, for revenue and also to show what the club was made of for potential buyers. But we knew getting past Oxford was never going to be a doddle. They were tough, full of hard players, none more so than Steve 'the Headband' Foster.

Fortunately it turned out to be one of those games where no matter what I tried, it came off. I was involved in everything, all over the pitch – tackling, passing, goals. I felt confident from the word go and early on I tried to take on the whole team, well five of them anyway. I picked the ball up from Nayim about fifteen yards outside their box and waltzed my way through the defence before cutting it back from the goal line. A pity their goalie got a hand to it. When it was shown on telly it was described as a 'scintillating run' as I 'threatened to tiptoe through the lot of them'. Cheers Motty.

We scored first, when Lineker and I worked a one-two into the box and the ball spun out of a challenge and broke to Gary Mabbutt who scored. Within twenty minutes we were two up. I stuck me head on a loose ball in the midfield and sent it through to Lineker who smashed a belter into the roof of the net. We should have been coasting then but they were battlers and got a good goal back before half-time to make it 2–1.

I got our third against Oxford about an hour into the match. I picked up the ball midway into their half and worked a neat one-two with Paul Walsh. I took the ball in me stride, which got me past the central defenders and then, as the keeper came out, I took it round him and banged it in from a tight angle. Big Steve Foster did his best to get to me but he was too late. As I ran off to celebrate I started shouting 'I'm the No. 1! I'm the No. 1!' I don't think Gary was too impressed. 'What's that all about?' 'Well, I am the No. 1.'

He looked at us as if to say, 'Are you?' He had been banging in most of the goals, I suppose.

Oxford still weren't out of it and with ten minutes to go they pulled another one back to make it 3–2. Seven minutes later we managed to settle it. Paul Allen cut along the edge of the box and slipped it through to me. There wasn't much room but I took a couple of touches and then cracked it home for 4–2. The relief was huge. You can see it on me face at the beginning of this chapter. We hadn't fancied going to the Manor Ground for a replay.

PORTSMOUTH – 16 FEBRUARY 1991

Pompey were a good team and we knew this wasn't going to be easy, especially as we were away. In circumstances like that, it is important to prepare properly. You don't want to do anything daft that could jeopardise your chances of taking another step towards Wembley. Do you?

I got a bit bored on the night before the game. I was rooming with Paul Stewart and next door was John Moncur and Steve Sedgley. There was a squash court in the hotel so I persuaded John to come down for a knockabout. We had to crawl along the floor and sneak behind furniture to get past Terry Venables but we made it and had about fifteen games, both going at it hard, trying to win. We eventually got to bed at about quarter to midnight but after about ten minutes I gave John a call in his room.

'Monty, are you feeling anything?'

'Yeah, me legs are killing us.'

'Mine too.'

They really were, I was aching, so I decided to have a bath. I thought it would help relax me but it only made things worse. I was in agony most of the night and can't have got much more than a couple of hours' sleep.

I didn't say a thing to the gaffer of course, but as I was putting me kit on I began to worry that I might pull a hamstring so I decided to put on heavy leg protectors. Throughout the whole of the first half I was total crap. Terrible. I could barely move me legs, I was so stiff. I certainly couldn't run anywhere, or jump. If Venables finds out, I thought, I'm screwed. Especially as they went in at the break one up.

Whose daft idea was it to weigh me down with that strapping? I can hardly get off the ground.

Much better. Back to me normal featherweight.

At half-time Terry asked if I was alright and I just said my legs were a little tired. He asked why, but I didn't tell him. I put it down to the leg protectors. 'So take them off.' I did and about five minutes into the second half I began to feel a bit fresher. From out on the right, Paul Allen whipped in a cross. I managed to get me head to it and it's gone into the top corner as you can see on the previous page. I was so relieved but I knew I wasn't out of the shit yet. I remember thinking, you got one, Paul, that's good, but you need to score again or the gaffer'll nail you.

To this day I don't think Gary Lineker knows why I didn't pass, especially as he made a great run to my left. Pat van den Hauwe played the ball over the top and picked it up with the defence running backwards. I did a little step-over trick I'd picked up from Chris Waddle and it sold the defender, who went right as I went left. I could see Gary was in a perfect position but I kept hold of it and knocked it into the bottom corner. It felt like I'd just about got away with me daftness from the night before. I was wrong.

NOTTS COUNTY – 10 MARCH 1991

My hernia went in training the day before the Notts County match. It hadn't felt right since the squash game, but I didn't admit that to the gaffer. I told Terry I was struggling and he sent me home. 'Rest up. I need you tomorrow.'

Next day Terry asked how I was feeling. 'Alright' I assured him, but in the warm-up I did me other one. 'There's no way I can play, Boss. Sorry.'

'You're going to have to.'

'But I'm in agony. I need an operation.'

'Just hold on, Gaz.' Then he rings up for the doctor to come down. 'See what you can do. We need him this afternoon.'

Eight injections later I couldn't feel a thing. I was totally numb. I think some of whatever they put into me must have gone to me head because towards the end of the first half I totally switched off on the edge of our box, the ball was nicked away from us and they scored a cracker.

We came out stronger in the second half and Nayim drew us level with a deflected shot early on, from my short corner. I was pleased I'd been involved in the goal. It helped make up a little bit for me mistake earlier in the game, but it wasn't enough. As the game wore on I started to worry about the damage I was doing to myself, because I couldn't feel anything, but I was still determined to try and make me mark. With less than ten minutes remaining I got my chance when the ball broke to me on the left of their box after a neat bit of passing between Sedgley and Mabbutt. I got in there just before Sedgley and curled it in.

'I think some of whatever they put into me must have gone to me head because towards the end of the first half I totally switched off on the edge of our box, the ball was nicked away from us and they scored a cracker.'

I knew that they wouldn't be able to come back after that. We were heading for the semi-final. I was so excited. We all were. You can see it on the faces when they jumped on top of us, which pretty much finished me off. If I wasn't fucked beforehand, I was after that. As the numbness wore off. I'd never felt pain like it in all me life. All I could do was stick on the halfway line, just about managing to move back and forth across the line to make sure I didn't play anyone onside. Paul Stewart covered my space for me.

The pain was getting worse and worse so I shuffled over to Terry on the bench. 'Get me off, Boss. I need an ambulance.' Only problem was, we'd used our subs so I had to stay put. When the final whistle blew I quickly applauded our fans and headed up the tunnel, walking as though I had been riding a horse for ten hours. There was an ambulance waiting for me but before I got in, Terry wanted a quick word with our physio. 'How long will it take to get over a double hernia?'

'He'll be ready to play again in about six weeks.'

'We can't do it then. We've got the semi-final in four.'

I was in absolute agony. 'Please let me have the op. I'll be back in three weeks. Properly fit. I promise.'

I had the operation next morning. I was determined to fulfil my promise and did everything I could to speed things up. I even shaved me own knackers before the operation to save time. When I woke up afterwards there was a woman sitting by my bed, holding me hand. 'Hi, who are you?' She said 'Give us ten.' 'Ten what?' 'Sit-ups.' 'But what about me stitches?' 'Terry Venables says you've got to be fit. So we've made the stitches extra tight. They won't come out.' I did ten and I was knackered and out of breath. 'Okay, I'll be back in an hour.'

So I was lying there, still a bit groggy, when I noticed me balls. They were massive, because of the op. I was dead excited so pressed the emergency bell for the nurse. When she came in all worried I pulled up me gown and said, 'Look at them!' She started to check them over, thinking there was something wrong. 'Do they hurt?' 'Nah, not really. But they are fucking massive aren't they. I had to show someone.' She thought it was funny but I did apologise for being so rude.

After about a week I was up on me feet and walking. I really wanted to get stuck into some training but the nurse said that I couldn't be discharged until I had been to the toilet. Seems they were worried I might do myself some more damage if I strained too hard. I hadn't been since the operation and I still didn't feel like it. So I tried to con her. Like I said, I was determined to do all I could to make the semi-final.

Someone had brought me a box of chocolates so I chewed up a few of them and spat them into the toilet, giving the bowl the old pebbledash look, and then called her into the room. 'There,' I said, looking all pleased with meself. 'I've been. Can I go now?' Although, being a nurse and all, she had probably seen everything under the sun, she didn't hang around to check too closely. Can't say I blame her. 'I'll get the forms ready so you can leave. It is a good job you went because it can go wrong and cause a lot of pain and problems.' That made me worry. I didn't need any setbacks with so little time before the semi, so I admitted what I had done. I asked if I could get a load of prunes which did the trick a few hours later.

'I knew that they wouldn't be able to come back after that. We were heading for the semi-final.'

ARSENAL – 14 APRIL 1991. THE SEMI-FINAL.

I started working on getting fit. John Sheridan was in charge of the physio side of things and Dave Bulter the training. Fuck me, he pushed us harder than he had ever done before. Loads of sprint repetitions and then sit-ups to strengthen the muscles in me groin. It was horrible because I was on my own, mornings and afternoons, and I could see the lads warming up on the other side of the field. I desperately wanted to be in that team. As a kid I had dreamt of walking up those Wembley steps as a winner and I didn't want to miss my chance. Fair play to Dave, he worked us hard and two days before the match I was ready to join the guys.

There was a lot of speculation as to whether I was going to make it or not. There was talk in the press that the Arsenal manager, George Graham, would have to change his tactics if he knew I was playing. So it was all a bit secret. Only, no one told me. I went to watch Luton play, I think it was the Wednesday before the match. I ended up chatting to some bloke in the lounge who was asking me about my injury and how I was getting on. I said I was feeling fit and he asked if I would be playing Saturday. 'That's the plan,' I told him. Afterwards I asked one of the Luton directors who I'd been speaking to. Turns out he was assistant manager at Arsenal. Smart move, Paul.

There was a brilliant atmosphere in the squad in the run-up to the semi-final. We were buzzing, everyone was up, laughing and joking. You sometimes find that teams in the FA Cup play a different game to their normal style, but we were confident that if we kept playing the same way we had been all season, we'd win. In the dressing room before the game Terry Venables let me speak to all the lads about how much this mattered. That was good of him.

The match started and we got a free kick after only about five minutes. You might know what happened next, but I never tire of talking about it. It's one of my very favourite football moments. It was thirty-five yards out but I was looking at the goal thinking, I can hit it from here. Probably because it was only Dave Seaman in goal. (Only joking, Dave.) So I was weighing up what to do, when Gary Lineker ran past and said, 'Have a go.' That settled it.

Seaman was lining up his wall, screaming at them to go left a bit, when I noticed Kevin Campbell shaking his head like he was saying, 'Don't worry about it. He's got no chance. It's too far out.' That spurred me on even more.

The gaffer wasn't exactly over-confident I would make it.

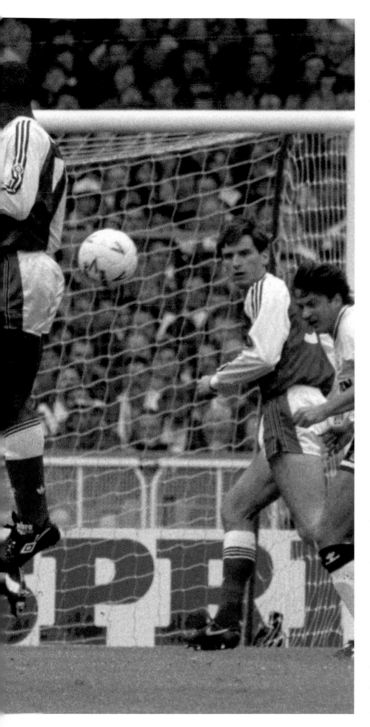

I gave it a crack and I'd never caught a ball like it before in my life. It was lovely. Schoolboys' Own stuff, as Barry Davies said on the telly. I think maybe I was a bit fortunate that Seaman tried to stretch over with his right to get it. If he had used his left he might have had more of a chance, but I still think the power would have beat him. The joy when it went in was incredible. I was screaming me head off. I ran to celebrate with Terry and the staff and subs because they had all been so supportive of me. Some of the lads on the bench used to stay back after training to help me get fit. I appreciated that and I wanted them to know it.

I was subbed with about twenty minutes to go. I had been running me nuts off and was knackered. We were 2–1 up then so it was still a bit nervy until Gary got his second. His first had been a classic toe-poke inside the six-yard box and the second is one of those that Dave Seaman would probably rather forget. Gary's shot sort of went through Dave's hands and into the net. But none of us cared about the quality of the goals. All that mattered was that we were in the final. I was convinced I was going to be walking up those steps just as I'd dreamed.

On the final whistle I ran straight to Paul Stewart. We'd spent a lot of time together and we were always talking about going to Wembley in the cup. He gave me a kiss. 'We're going, Paul.' Then I ran over to where me dad and mates were. I'd organised a load of coaches to come down from Dunston and I was trying to point them out to Gary. I couldn't see them, mind, but knowing they were there in the crowd was all that mattered.

NOTTINGHAM FOREST – 18 MAY 1991. THE FINAL.

I was way too hyped for the match but there was nothing anyone could have done to calm me down. The night before I couldn't sleep; I was kicking lampshades pretending they were footballs. Eventually someone called the doctor who gave us a Valium. That did the trick, but it was short-lived. It was the FA Cup final. It was everything I wanted. I was young, and when we arrived at Wembley the noise and the flags and the buzz got to me.

Before the game I said to the lads that I was going to ask Princess Diana for a kiss, but they didn't believe me. So we were in the presentation line-up and it came to my turn. 'Can I have a kiss, your Majesty?' I didn't really know how to address her. She said yes so I made a bit of a move to get in there but she stuck out her hand instead. Oh well. Better than nothing. She was lovely. Afterwards I heard that the Queen had put a stop on me meeting Diana again, just in case I went for another kiss or put me arm around her like I did when I met Margaret Thatcher after the World Cup.

The game kicked off and I felt good, in control. Then within the first minute or so the ball broke between me and Garry Parker. We were both fully committed but I over stretched and went right over it and smacked me studs off his chest. It was an accident, but it was a shocker, reckless and stupid, no doubt about it. Garry just got up and got on with it which was good of him. He was a quality player in every sense.

I think I'd probably have been sent off if it had happened later in the match, but because it was early, in a final, the ref was lenient but he did have a word with me, telling me to calm down. People say in hindsight that it would have been better for me if he had produced a red card then, because then I wouldn't have made the second challenge and things would have been very different. I don't agree. I have always been happy with the way my career turned out.

So that was a bad enough start, but then it all really went wrong in the fifteenth minute.

Gary Charles got the ball on the edge of our box. He was in a bit of space and I instantly felt that if I didn't stop him, he'd be through the gap and in on goal. Van den Hauwe was behind me but I wasn't sure he would get there in time. As Gary picked the ball up he's taken a bit of a heavy touch which took him across me and made me check my

run. So I was a bit off balance when I took a swipe for the ball. I've missed it by a mile and cut him down. It was a dreadful challenge. I know that. It wasn't malicious but it was still awful. No excuses.

As I made the tackle I felt something go in my knee but it didn't feel too bad, not right, but not a disaster. It was hurting but I thought it was going to be okay. I got back on me feet, but was careful not to twist the knee. Going back into the wall, I made sure to walk in straight lines. Stuart Pearce then banged in the free kick to put them one up.

I was still being very careful not to put any strain on my knee, but I needed to find out if I'd be able to carry on. So at the restart I called for the ball. 'Give it here. I need it.' The ball was played across my left side and as I've turned towards it, that was it. I knew immediately that something terrible had happened. My knee was shaking.

Dave Butler came charging on, followed by a stretcher. Dave said there was no way I could continue. He thought it might be the medial ligament. I asked how long I'd be out.

'At least a month?' I said.

'No, a bit longer than that.' I could feel myself welling up.

'Three months?'

'Might be more.'

'Not six months?'

'No, a year.'

As they were stretchering me off I had one last look at those steps. I never did walk up them as a winner.

I was taken straight to the hospital where, because the match went to extra time, I got to see the end of it and Des Walker scoring the own goal that won us the cup, unlucky for him. Afterwards the lads brought the trophy to the hospital which was brilliant of them but I didn't feel I deserved it. Even though I'd probably done more than most to get Spurs to Wembley I felt I'd let them all down when it mattered most. It was to be my last ever match for Tottenham.

RECOVERY

Two days after the final I was meant to be heading to Rome, to finalise the move to Lazio that had been brewing for a while. I decided to go because the money was great and because Spurs were going to get £8.5 million. Terry Venables told me he wanted us to stay but that he would hate to stand in the way of a move to Italy. Playing on the Continent, he said, was an amazing opportunity and as I was still a young kid with loads to learn, Lazio would be perfect. He also said that if I got bored or didn't like it, he would buy us back. So that felt okay to me.

Everything was put on hold, however, until the Italians were certain I was fully fit. It was going to take months. My knee obviously required an operation and after that was done I

had to put in some hard graft to get back in shape. But not before I had a bit of a break in Portugal to recuperate, naturally.

Everything went well over that summer and I even managed to say my proper goodbyes and thanks to the Spurs fans when I pulled on the strip again for the Charity Shield in August. I didn't play, of course, but it felt good to be part of it even if the scar on me knee was a constant reminder of what had happened the last time I was on that pitch.

Not long after that I went over to Rome to meet the fans and everything looked to be on course for the transfer. Then, at the end of September, I went up to Newcastle to sort a few things out, but instead got sorted out meself. I was in a nightclub when some bloke clobbered us and down I went, messing up me knee again. It was the worst feeling imaginable. After all the hard work, I knew I was back to square one.

I wanted the same surgeon who had looked after me before to take a look so Jimmy drove me down to London that night. I went to see John Sheridan first, the Spurs' physio, to tell him what had happened. He was as upset as I was. Mr Browett, the surgeon, was having his Sunday lunch when we called but he operated that afternoon. He was brilliant.

So it was going to be another seven months before there was any chance I could play again. It was incredibly depressing but there was no choice but to start my recuperation all over again. The Lazio board were patient though, they were getting reports and scans and Spurs sent them videos of me training and eventually kicking a ball again.

The 1991/92 season finished and I was just about fit again but I still hadn't played a full match. I knew Lazio would need to see me play ninety minutes to be finally convinced but by then all the lads had gone off for the summer, so I went round to the Spurs apprentices and asked them to hang on another day, because Lazio were coming over for one last look at me. I said I'd pay them £50 each if they'd turn up and they all did. A whole bunch of the Lazio staff were there and I remember scoring a goal past Ian Walker. We were videoing the match and when the ball went in I turned to the camera, looked straight at it and shouted. 'I'm back!'

CHAPTER 5

ISLAND HOLIDAY

ITALIA '90:
GROUP STAGE

We'd flown out to our World Cup camp in Sardinia on 25 May 1990. The plan was to get acclimatised to the heat, play one last warm-up match and generally work together as a squad to build up the team spirit. Not that we really needed it. From the very beginning the feeling in the camp was unbelievable and stayed that way right through to the end. It was frightening how tight we were, and it wasn't just the lads who were playing, everyone contributed. Even the boys who knew they weren't going to get a game. That impressed me. I am not sure I would have coped as well.

In my mind the World Cup was like one big holiday, a holiday that I actually wanted to be on and which I never wanted to end. I couldn't take things as seriously as maybe the others did. It felt like I was back playing with me mates at Redheugh Boys' Club, only the facilities were a bit better – table tennis, a swimming pool, golf courses, tennis courts.

It was me twenty-third birthday two days after we arrived in Sardinia. I'd already had the best birthday present ever, just being there, but the lads decided I should have a cake. That was nice of them, if only I'd gotten to eat it. I was by the pool relaxing, when bang, Chris Waddle smacked it straight in me face. Everyone started joining in and we had a right laugh.

'I'd already had the best birthday present ever, just being there, but the lads decided I should have a cake.'

The last warm-up game before the tournament began was against Tunisia, in Tunis. We flew there from Sardinia. I wish we hadn't bothered, and judging by the size of the crowd, so did the Tunisians. I tried to play a back pass to Peter Shilton but it was a shocker and their forward picked it up and scored. For the rest of the match I played like shit. I didn't want the ball in case I screwed up again. I couldn't shake off my mistake. I kept thinking, that's it, you are not going to play, you've blown any chance of making the starting line-up against Ireland.

At the end of the match I was very low, and it was at times like this that Bobby Robson showed how brilliant he was. He recognised the state I was in and knew me enough by then to realise I would let it eat away at me, so he put his arm around me and said, 'Don't worry about it, Paul. You'll be fine. ' That was all I needed.

A warm-up match against Uruguay. I can't imagine where a young lad like me learned bad language.

I was incredibly lucky coming into that squad for Italia '90. I was one of the youngest, if not the youngest, and I was surrounded by an unbelievable group of players, people like Terry Butcher, Peter Beardsley, Chris Waddle and Bryan Robson, all in their prime. They looked after me, playing to their different strengths. I could play the one-twos with Peter and Chris, developing my fluent game, Butcher would tell me where to go and how to defend when we had to and Robson minded my back. 'Anything that comes in the air, I'll get. You leave them alone. I'll take the knocks and play your own game, Gazza. I don't mind if I pick up an injury. You've got your career ahead of you.'

Having the England captain say that to you is incredible. I felt ten feet taller. Especially after all the knocks he'd had over his career. In later years, whenever I got an injury I'd call him up. 'What now?' he'd ask. 'I've done me arm in. How long will that take?' 'Fucking hell, Gazza, it'll take about four and a half weeks.' Next one. 'I've broke me leg.' 'Fibula or tibia?' I'd tell him and he'd let me know how long to expect. Pretty much any bone, Robbo had been there and broken it.

CARRY ON CAMPING

The training at camp was hard, but it was good. During the actual tournament if you had played it was only light training the following morning, but if you hadn't been involved then it was full pelt all the way through. Poor old Terry Butcher got a clatter in the face during one knockabout and had to be looked after by Doctor Gascoigne. I am not sure he ever properly recovered. Each day we were getting stronger and better, but we still had time for laughs and jokes.

There was no drinking allowed, not during those first couple of weeks, but that's not to say it never happened. Wives and girlfriends had been allowed to visit for a couple of days, before the tournament got underway. It was another element of the team-building.

Only problem was, I was single at the time and got the hump a bit. So I decided I needed a drink to cheer me up – without Bobby Robson knowing. I hit on a brilliant plan, thanks to a frothy cappuccino. I ordered a load of Baileys from the bar, put it in a cup and scraped the foam off me coffee. Now who said I was daft?

I took a few sips and began to feel better almost immediately. Some of the lads were playing a game of charades with the girls and they had tried to persuade me to join in. Bollocks to that, I had told them earlier, but now that I was feeling merrier I decided to give it a go. 'I've got one,' I shouted and they all cheered. 'Two words. Fuck off.' Terry Butcher chased us halfway round the hotel. 'I'm gonna kill you, Gascoigne. Swearing in front of my wife.' It was hilarious. He didn't catch me, thank God, and we had a good laugh about it afterwards.

Terry and I had another run in at the camp, and this time he did get the better of me. We were each given a bar of chocolate every evening, for energy I guess, and Chris Waddle and I used to wolf ours down straight off. One night I fancied some more and I started to wonder who might not eat his chocolate until the morning. Who would be that dull? Terry Butcher? I sneaked into his room while he and Chris Woods were asleep, opened the fridge and sure enough, my instincts were spot on.

I was just reaching for the bar when I heard a voice behind me, 'Who the fuck is that!' I grabbed the chocolate and ran out the door. Terry started chasing me down the corridor while Woods went the other way. I knew I was quicker than Terry so I was feeling pretty pleased with meself when I rounded a corridor and there was Chris. He grabbed me and stuck an orange in my face. I went to bed sticky and still hungry.

Not for long though. Waddler and I found a treasure chest of wallets and pens and that sort of thing that the England staff used to give out as gifts. And the rest of the chocolate. It was stashed away in one of the hotel rooms. When I say we found it, that's not actually true. It was Peter Beardsley and he came to our room and told Chris and me. Daft bugger. He knew he's made a mistake as soon as he said it. He kept pleading 'Don't do anything, don't tell anyone.' He was worried he'd be in the shit. 'We'll keep it to ourselves,' we assured him.

As soon as Peter left, me and Chris were straight there. We pinched loads of gear. I had about forty bars of chocolate under me bed. Peter must have heard us because he came in as we were about to make our getaway. 'I've got nowt to do with this. Nowt.' Chris and me were pissing ourselves. Everybody knew it was us but nobody said anything and the next day the door was locked.

On one of our days off we went down to the beach to sunbathe. David Platt had joined the squad – more of that later – and ever since he'd arrived he hadn't stopped going on about Doug Ellis, the Aston Villa owner and Platty's boss. It was all, 'Doug Ellis has the best yacht. Doug Ellis is going to do this. Doug Ellis is going to do that. Doug Ellis had installed the best pitch. Doug Ellis has flown to the moon.' By lunchtime we'd had a few drinks, although we shouldn't have, and I decided it was time to take the piss.

There was a big-ass yacht anchored about three hundred yards off the beach and when I saw it I shouted, 'Ooh, look. Dougie and his boat!' I started to swim out to it and a few of the lads followed, mainly because I said that they would probably have loads of drink on board. As we got nearer I was calling out, 'Oh Dougie. Oh Dougie. Where are you?' Just then a bloke peered over the side. 'Hello Paul.' Fuck me, it was Doug Ellis.

About eight of us clambered on board, including Gary Lineker's missus. We must have got through about thirty bottles of champagne and all his food. It was brilliant. At one point I leapt on Mrs Lineker for a laugh and we both tumbled over the side and into the ocean. Fortunately she saw the funny side but I am not sure Gary did.

By the time we had to leave I was smashed. We were swimming back and I was about a hundred yards from shore when I began to get tired. I decided the best thing to do was take a deep breath, dive to the seabed, give myself a moment to relax, then push up and swim back as fast as I could. Yeah I know, not the smartest decision I've made, but I was pissed. As I was coming back up I must have got turned around because after resurfacing and swimming hard I looked up expecting to see the shore but discovered I was heading out in the wrong direction. I was beginning to struggle and I panicked a bit. It was quite frightening. I started to wave my arms in the air and luckily enough a little dinghy with an outboard motor turned up. It was Gary Lineker and another bloke. 'Get in you daft bastard,' he said. When I looked up it was Nigel Kennedy, the violinist. 'Give us a tune then, Nige,' I said. 'Handel's Water Music?' he laughed. I didn't have a clue what he was on about.

'There was no drinking allowed, not during those first couple of weeks, but that's not to say it never happened.'

IRELAND

Our first match in the World Cup was against Ireland. It was a hot night and I just wanted to get through the game with no problems.

As we walked out on to the pitch it was a bit weird seeing Jack Charlton, their manager, on the touchline. Having worked with him at Newcastle I had a fair idea what his team talk would have been. 'If you get a chance, sort out that little bastard Gascoigne.' That didn't bother me though. We knew beforehand that it would be a tough game, and it was.

I hadn't been nervous in the run-up to the game because I knew we had another two matches to go if anything went wrong, but standing there as the national anthem was being played, suddenly the nerves kicked in. I could hardly sing a word. I opened and closed me

mouth, pretending, until the last bit. I did manage to belt out the final words 'God Save the Queen.' The pride I felt at that moment was incredible.

It was a tense game, not surprising really as it was the first match of the World Cup for both teams. I remember going mental at the ref. Ireland had a free kick and because I was second in the wall it was my responsibility to make sure we were lined up correctly, protecting one side of the goal. Shilts was screaming at me, 'Sort it out. Move to the left. Move to the left.' But I couldn't hear him because at the same time the ref was shouting 'Come back, come back.' That's when I lost it. 'Fuck off, ref!' Not very clever but I think he understood the pressure everyone was under and let it go. Mind you, if he'd booked me then things might have been different later on.

Throughout the match Ray Houghton was after me like a little terrier, snapping at me heels and trying to put me off me game. It worked, I didn't play that well and it wasn't a classic match. Gary Lineker scored early on and then Kevin Sheedy equalled with a belter in the second half, and that was it. But at least we were underway, if not very impressively

We had a couple of days off after that match and I started thinking that back home I would normally go for a drink to relax. The next day we were all lying on the beach reading and chatting, but all I could think about was having a sneaky bevvy. There was no way I could have a beer or a glass of wine or anything like that – way too obvious. Then it came to me: a pina colada. I left

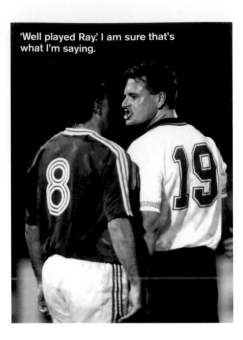

'Well played Ray.' I am sure that's what I'm saying.

the lads soaking up the sun and ran up to the little cocktail hut where the barman produced a drink with the works hanging off it – fruit, umbrella, the lot. Del Boy would have loved it. I had just started sipping away when Bobby Robson appeared. Shit, I thought. He's going to nick me and I'll be on the plane home in an hour.

'What's that you've got there, Gaz?'

'Eh...a vanilla milkshake, Boss.'

'Nice, can I have a taste?'

'Sure thing, here.' I was definitely screwed now.

He liked it. 'I'll have the same.'

I had one last chance. 'Yeah,' I said to the barman, trying desperately to wink without the gaffer seeing me. 'A vanilla milkshake. You know, A...Vanilla...Milk...Shake.'

He cottoned on, God bless him, and produced an actual vanilla milkshake. Sir Bobby had a taste, and then says to me, 'Can I try yours again?'

He took a sip and looked puzzled. 'Mine's not the same.' Then turning to the barman he asked, 'I know what it is! Can I have an umbrella, cherries and a straw please, like his.' What a relief! Although I shouldn't have told the lads… When I came back down from me room a little bit later, the barman was mixing up about twenty pina coladas for the boys on the beach.

HOLLAND

Next up was Holland. They had some team – Rijkaard, Koeman, Van Basten – but again I wasn't nervous. For me, the bigger the challenge, the better. The player I was most excited about facing was Ruud Gullit. I'd loved watching him in the 1988 European Championships, when he scored with a bullet header, his dreadlocks flying all over the place. I always wondered what they felt like. Now was my chance to find out. We were tussling for the ball in the corner and it went out for a throw in. Just as we were both straightening up I had a quick tug of his hair, just to satisfy my curiosity. I think he was a bit shocked and he turned round as if he was going to have a go at me, but when I gave him a big grin, he smiled back.

Although it was nil-all, the match went really well for us. Much better than the Ireland performance. We changed our

Hairing past Gullit. Gettit?

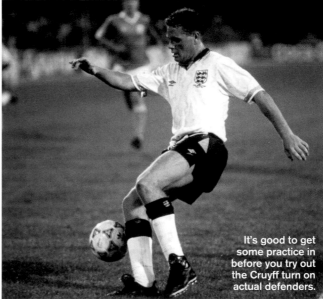

It's good to get some practice in before you try out the Cruyff turn on actual defenders.

ISLAND HOLIDAY

91

formation, with Mark Wright playing sweeper brilliantly, and it worked. They hardly had a sniff at goal and we were the better team.

I made some good runs and great passes but the moment that stood out the most was giving them the old Cruyff turn. Talk about coals to Newcastle. I'd seen the great man do it on telly when I was seven and I practised it for years until I mastered it. Down in their left-hand corner I turned two of their defenders inside out and squared the ball to Lineker who missed by a whisker. It would have been extra sweet if that had gone in.

After the match a few of us sneaked out for a beer or two. Well, we were excited, we'd just mullered (okay, drew nil-all with) the European champions. We were in a bar having a right laugh, arm wrestling locals and generally mucking around, when we heard sirens coming our way. We thought the gaffer had realised we had sneaked out and had sent the police to fetch us!

We all legged it back to the hotel but we were all still in a really good mood so a few of us ended up in the room I shared with Waddler. Bryan Robson was there and we were mucking about. As he tried to tip me off the bed, it slipped from his grasp and smashed his toe. The shit hit the fan then. We'd just lost our captain to a daft bit of nonsense. Pretty much the next day Bryan was off back home – the reason given being that an old Achilles injury had come back during the Holland game. Oops.

Next morning we were relaxing by the pool, trying not to think of what had happened. Bobby Robson was furious and who could blame him? Anyway, I remember one of the lads saying that the gaffer was on his way down so we should try to cheer him up. I went into the bathroom and wrapped toilet roll around my head and arm as if I was bandaged. When the gaffer saw me he exploded. 'Bloody hell! What now?' He saw the funny side, I think, when I started to peel all the paper off.

Then I decided to see who could dive furthest off the diving board. I took a run and jumped and as I did I caught my right toe and it started to bleed. Loads. There was blood in the pool. The gaffer definitely didn't see the funny side of this one. 'I can't believe it. I've lost my captain, with his left toe, and now my other midfield man with his right.' I tried to calm him down by saying it was okay and would only need a plaster. At the next training session it was killing us but I didn't let on. I reckoned the boss had been through enough.

EGYPT

If you look hard enough I'm in the background here, having just delivered the perfect ball, of course.

Our 1–0 win in the final group match put us top of the table. I was pretty happy – my holiday was going to last a bit longer. I put over the free kick which Mark Wright headed in for the goal and as it hit the back of the net I thought this is the moment my World Cup really starts. Then one of the best things in the whole tournament happened. Peter Beardsley jumped up off the bench to give us a hug. I thought that was fantastic. He hadn't been in the team for the Holland match and was on the bench for this one but he wasn't sulking – he was the first person jumping up to celebrate. To me, that said everything about the incredible team spirit we had.

We were ready to leave our island hideaway and move on to the serious business on the mainland.

CHAPTER 6

ON TO THE MAINLAND

ITALIA '90:
KNOCKOUT STAGE

BELGIUM

Bobby Robson showed us videos of Belgium playing before we met them in the first knockout round. I'd be up against a bloke called Enzo Scifo and as I watched him I knew I was going to have me hands full. I did. He was brilliant during the game, hitting the inside of the post in the second half with a shot that had Shilton flapping at air. Right from the outset I tried to niggle him a little, just to wind him up, joking around to distract him. Even still, he was getting the better of me, so as the match headed towards extra time I decided to remind him I was still around.

Me leg! Me leg!

I went in for a hefty challenge on Scifo, fair I think, and he hit the deck, squealing like he's dying. I was getting fed up with all the diving I was seeing in the matches – I'd never really come across it before – so I sort of took the piss out of him, pretending I'd hurt me knee and was in agony.

It wasn't quite so funny when the ref booked us, mind. As it was my first of the tournament I wasn't too worried though. I certainly didn't think for a second it was going to play a major part in the rest of me life

Bryan Robson didn't play in the match of course, he was back in England, so Steve McMahon was in the midfield alongside me and Waddle. Steve ran his nuts off in that game. He was brilliant. He covered for me, tackled for me and tried to give me space to play. I wasn't surprised when he was subbed with about fifteen minutes to go. He must have been exhausted.

The match went into extra time, with both sides having chances, and as the clock ticked down it looked as though it was going to penalties. I was totally knackered, running on self-will and the pure buzz of the World Cup. But at least I knew they had to be as tired as we were, so I decided to give it one last go. I picked up the ball in our half and focused on getting ahead of the defenders, arms spread out to shield the ball. I was trying to get as far down the pitch as I could but I was brought down. Free kick.

I was standing over the ball as the boys were moving into the box thinking, I could just give it a go. Even if I don't score, I thought, the keeper might get a touch and it could rebound to one of our players. There were only seconds left so I made up me mind to have a pop.

The gaffer obviously knew what I was thinking because just then, as I was lining up the shot, I heard screaming from the bench. I didn't really want to look up because I knew who it was. 'Chip it in, Gazza. Get it in the box. Don't do anything stupid.'

I did what I was told and drifted it towards the far post. David Platt, brought in to replace Robbo, picked up the flight of the ball perfectly. As it came over his shoulder he spun and cracked it home. It was incredible. That one goal pretty much made Platty's career. Without me it was straight back to non-league football for him – that's what I like to tell him anyway. It's not true of course. He would have made the Third Division, easy.

When the ball hit the back of the net all the players ran to Platt to celebrate but I was thinking about McMahon, how he had done all that running for me and how he wasn't on the pitch to join in. So I ran over to the bench first to give him a big hug, to say, 'That goal is as much about you as anyone else.'

The atmopshere in the dressing room afterwards showed how good the team spirit was within the squad. We were all happy that we had won, obviously, but me and Steve McMahon were making the most noise, jumping around in the bath, splashing and generally carrying on. Shilts tells us to calm down, saying that we hadn't won anything yet and Steve

tells him to fuck off. This type of thing is normal and I think Shilts was just trying to show his experience, he'd been there before after all. But it was a bit unnecessary and caused some unpleasantness. However, it was pretty much the first and last difficult moment of the whole campaign. The important point was that it was over very quickly. We were too close knit to let small things get in the way of winning the trophy.

I didn't really think about the win the next day. It took a couple of days before it kicked in. We were in the quarter-finals of the World Cup. Even thinking about it today gives me goose bumps and a lump in me throat. That was about the only time in the whole tournament I took a moment to meself to think about what we were doing, where we had got to, what we were hoping to achieve, what it all meant. I began to think how this was my time, how I didn't want to share it with anyone else apart from me family. I used to call home after each game and speak to me dad. 'You did well today, son. Congratulations. Keep at it. We're proud of you.' That was more than enough for me.

To keep our minds off the next match the England staff put on a race night in the hotel. One of those ones where they show videos of races and you bet on them. Our physio, Fred Street, had organised it and before it all started he called me aside. 'Listen Gaz, in the fifth race, back number five: Run High. Don't tell anyone else.' 'Sure thing, Boss.'

Pretty much the only two people I didn't tell were Lineker and Shilton. There was a lot of betting going on the whole time in the camp, just small stuff to keep things interesting, and it was those two who ran the book. It was the same thing that night. So the race comes up and Run High is at 6–1. I put fifty quid on and a number of the other lads did the same. Just before the race started, Lineker turned to me, looking a bit worried. 'Do you know something?' 'No Gary, nowt. I've just got a feeling, that's all.'

The race starts and I am shouting at the screen, 'Go on, come on', acting as if I was the jockey, with the reins in me hand and giving it the whip. Waddler joins in and then so do the rest of them. It was brilliant. When it won, poor Shilts nearly fell off his seat. Between him and Lineker, they were set to lose about two-and-a-half grand. Shilts disappeared up to his room and after we'd confessed to Gary we couldn't decide whether it was best to tell Shilton now, or wait until the morning. Eventually it was agreed to let him know. I can't remember who went up, but the next thing we knew Shilts was charging down the stairs shouting he knew something was up and he was going to kill us all. We couldn't move for pissing ourselves with laughter.

CAMEROON

As the quarter-final approached the more press attention we got, the more interviews we were asked for, the more scrutiny we came under. Journalists weren't allowed in the hotel but they kept trying to get photos on the sly, hiding up in trees, that sort of thing. The way Bobby Robson dealt with it all helped me an awful lot. He seemed to take everything in his stride and the nearer we got to the final, the more I listened to him. Well, sort of.

The night before the Cameroon match, a few of the boys, and me needless to say, fancied a quick pint to relieve the tension so we sneaked out and found a quiet little bar. We really did only have one, maybe two, but no more, then it was back home. We were sure we wouldn't have been missed. Wrong. The gaffer was waiting by the hotel entrance. Shit. We dived behind a wall and tried to work out what to do. At this stage it was Chris Waddle, me and John Barnes. Barnsey reckoned our best bet was to climb the wall and quick as a flash he was over. What he didn't realise was that there was a twenty foot drop on the other side. All Chris and I heard was 'Aaaah. Boomph.'

'Let's try the side gate,' Chris suggested. Good plan. It was open and we made it to the lift without being seen. Brilliant, until the lift stopped on the first floor, the doors opened and there was the gaffer... 'Get to bed. I'll speak to you two tomorrow.' I was shitting myself. I thought I really had blown it this time. In our room I was upset that I had pushed it too far after all the other daft stuff and pleaded with Chris to do something. 'Please speak to him, Chris. Please get me out of this.'

Good on Chris. He had the balls to go and have a word with the gaffer, to tell him what had actually been going on and say that I was just a young lad and not to give me too hard a time. I really appreciated that. I think Bobby Robson understood, because he ended up being quite lenient on us.

In the stadium the next day the dressing rooms were about fifty yards apart with a long tunnel up to the pitch. First Bobby Robson gave us his team talk and then Terry Butcher took over. He always got incredibly worked up, screaming at us with real passion. 'This is England. This my house. No one comes in here and messes with my house!'

We were ready. We opened the dressing room door to go out for the match and all we could hear was singing coming along the corridor. It was the Cameroon team and as they

approached it got louder and louder. In the tunnel it was almost deafening. I kept me head down as we lined up waiting to walk out. Just as we began to move I looked up...and up and up. The bloke next to me was massive. When I looked back down again I noticed his boots with great big long studs. Their overall presence was terrifying. But then Terry Butcher started screaming again and we all started getting into it, ready to go out and get stuck in.

We'd seen enough of Cameroon in the tournament to know they were a good team. They'd beaten the holders Argentina in the first match so there was no chance of us being complacent. But I did feel confident. They played the ball well, but so did we. I kept thinking that all we needed to do was to match them at their own game and we'd have enough extra to get through.

I started well, putting in loads of skills which were coming off and I was pleased with how the game was going, especially in the twenty-fifth minute when Stuart Pearce broke down the left and put in a perfect cross on to David Platt's head. 1–0.

It stayed like that until half-time and then, about fifteen minutes into the second half, the ball was played through to Roger Milla in our box. I put my foot out to block it and over he went. Penalty. 1–1. Four minutes later it was even worse when they scored a really smart goal to go in front. I felt it was all my fault, having let them back into the match. And to add to our problems they were

beginning to play really well, closing us down fast, while the heat was getting to us in a big way.

For about five minutes after they scored the second I couldn't get it out of me head that I was going to get hammered for giving that penalty away. But I managed to pull myself together, saying over and over, 'Stop it Paul, there is plenty of time left.' I had faith that Lineker would score from anything that came his way. He was lethal. And on top of that we

had Chris Waddle and Peter Beardsley to make things happen.

Time was running out though. With less than ten minutes to go I floated a free kick over from the left and after the ball bobbled around a bit it broke to Lineker. Just as he was about to move in on goal his legs were swept away from behind. Penalty. Gary slotted the spot kick away perfectly. I thought their heads might go down then, thinking that their chance had gone. Far from it, they kept battling and when the match went into extra time they had a couple of good chances.

At the end of the first fifteen minutes I picked up the ball in the centre of midfield. Lineker was about forty yards away but I clocked his run and nailed a great ball. I knew that pass, I'd been making it since I was seventeen years old. I was on me toes, watching his movement, and I timed it just right. He slipped the ball past the keeper and was brought down again... As Gary stepped up to take the penalty I was watching from around the halfway line, praying that he would score. In my mind, everything seemed to hang on that spot kick. Somehow I felt I'd got my honour back with that pass, but if it didn't count towards a goal, there was no point. Gary had too much class to blow it and he didn't.

When the final whistle went I sprinted over to our bench and gave Bobby Robson a big hug. We were in the World Cup semi-final and I was more pleased for the gaffer than anyone else. He'd taken a lot of flak from the press even before we'd flown out to Sardinia – talk about how he had let England down by accepting a new job after the tournament. What a load of rubbish. It was the FA that screwed up, not Sir Bobby. After that, there had been crap written about him eyeing up the players' wives when they had been over. It was all just nonsense and he had handled it incredibly well. All he cared about was his team and winning the World Cup for his country.

I remember when he told me about the stories involving him and the players' wives. He was upset by it and just wanted to share it with someone. We were walking along the road and he was pointing at the story in the paper. 'Just look at this. Look at it. They're saying I'm looking at ladies' backsides.' He was so incensed he wasn't paying attention to where we were. Walking just in front of us was a group of wives. I better stop and have a look at the papers and see what he's on about, I thought, because if they get a picture of us right now, we're really up shit creek!

WEST GERMANY

The night before the semi-final, at around 10.30 p.m., as Chris was dozing off, I was lying on my bed unable to sleep. I could hear someone playing tennis outside, so I got dressed and went down there. Two Americans were on the court. 'Hi, I'm Paul. Can I have a game?' It was me against the two of them. I'm working hard, getting hot and sweaty, when after about twenty minutes I heard a familiar Geordie accent, 'Gascoigne! Gascoigne! What the hell are you doing?' It was the gaffer. I knew I was in trouble but he walks past me and up to the two blokes. 'Excuse me, do you not know who he is? Do you understand he's got the most important game of his life tomorrow? And you're playing bloody tennis with him!' They were clueless, they had no idea what he was on about.

As he was shouting at them I dropped my racket and bolted. I got back to my room, waking Chris up when I banged the door. He asked what was going on. 'I've been playing tennis, but the gaffer caught us and now he's going off on one.' I jumped into bed just before the knocking on the door started. 'Chris, tell him I'm sleeping.' So he goes to the door and tries his best but of course it doesn't work. 'Sleeping! He's just been playing bloody tennis!' He walked in and pulled the sheet off me. 'Gascoigne, I will see you in the morning.'

Next day I was certain I was going to be dropped, but Chris kept reassuring me. 'Nah, you'll be alright. He won't drop you. But I can't believe you were playing tennis. I knew you were mad, Gazza, but not that mad.' As I was heading towards the pre-match meeting, at around noon, the gaffer called me over. 'Gascoigne, you are playing tonight.' I felt instantly better. 'And you're playing against the best player in the world.' 'No,' I said. 'He is.' The gaffer just looked at the ground and shook his head.

I never liked to over analyse the opposition – that wasn't my style – I needed to keep my appetite fresh. But I'd heard all about Lothar Matthaus. He was lethal, with some shot on him and I knew he was going to be a handful. The way I looked at it, it was just him versus me. The other players could look after their own jobs. I respected Matthaus hugely, but I wasn't frightened of him.

As we were leaving the dressing room to line up in the tunnel, the weirdest thing happened. There was an old bloke there who I didn't recognise. He approached and

introduced himself. 'Mr Gascoigne. My name is Gianni Agnelli. I own Juventus. I want you to come and play for me.'

What? I was about to play the most important game of me life and I was getting tapped up. I didn't know how to respond. 'Eh, thank you. Can I speak to you later?'

'Of course. Good luck in the match.' That was it, he was gone. I did speak to him later and it turned out the deal was he wanted me to sign for Roma first! Juventus would pay for that, so that I could learn the language, the style of play, and then move on to Juve afterwards. 'I can't do that,' I explained. 'If I play for Roma and I like the fans and they like me, then I'll want to stay. I'm loyal.' And that was the end of that.

The semi-final against West Germany was, I would say, the best game I've ever played for England. I nearly scored very early on with a beauty of a strike. I was certain it was bound for the top corner and I was on the brink of congratulating myself on what a great goal it was when the keeper got his hand to it. It was disappointing, but it gave me a load of confidence. We were on top and playing well.

Then into the second half they went one nil up. I couldn't believe it. It was a fluke goal, a deflection off Paul Parker that looped over Shilton, but it was still a goal. I felt like crying. All I could think about was that I was going home. It wasn't about the final, or being one down, it was that the party was over. It only stayed with me for a minute or two before the roar of the fans picked me up and I was back in the game.

Our supporters were phenomenal. The noise was deafening but the game was dragging on and time was running out. Then the ball came to Paul Parker on the right and he launched it into the box. It fell kindly for Lineker and he scuffed his shot, but who cares. It conned the keeper and we were level and in with a shout.

We were into extra time, our third in nine days. This photo is just at the end of the ninety minutes. You'll notice no one is actually looking at the gaffer. We're all miles away, knackered and trying to get ourselves psyched for the next thirty minutes of play. So Bobby Robson starts screaming, 'Listen in! Listen in!' He eventually managed to bring us all together and we focused on what he was saying.

The Germans came at us strong, but I think we were looking the better team. Then disaster struck for me. I got the ball in the centre circle and bundled my way forward. Then, as Matthaus tried to nick it off me I nudged the ball out of his reach, but overran it. I had to stretch as Thomas Berthold came across. I was giving one hundred and ten per cent. It was the World Cup semi-final and I didn't want to give them anything for free. To this day I honestly don't think I touched him, but down he went, rolling around as if in agony. He must've done more damage with his theatrics than he got in the actual tackle.

I was foaming, but I went over to check on him to show there was nothing malicious in it. I didn't want to get booked. I'd been thinking about that a lot before the game. I crouched down to make sure he was okay and at that stage I wasn't thinking I was in trouble. There was nothing in the challenge. Then everything turned to slow motion. I straightened up and turned to the ref. He's gone for his pocket. Suddenly I can't hear anything. The world just stops apart from the bloke in black. My eyes follow his hand, to the pocket, then out with the card. There it is, raised above my head.

It took a few seconds and then it hit me. I wasn't going to play in the World Cup final. I was told that the ref later said that if he'd realised I had already been booked he wouldn't have brought the card out. Not much good to me now! The world started up again. I looked at the crowd, I looked at Lineker, and I couldn't hold it back. I started to cry. At that moment I just wanted to be left alone, I didn't want to talk to anyone or see anyone. My bottom lip was like a helicopter pad. I was devastated.

Then I heard our fans. They were incredible. My eyes swept across the pitch to the team, exhausted but still giving it their all. I thought, fuck that, if I am not going I want to help the guys get there. All the self-pity went out the window. I was determined to give everything I had.

Over the last twenty minutes I got forward, ran back, made challenges. As the game went on we dug deeper than they did and got stronger. I remember Chris Waddle had an unbelievable shot from the edge of their box. One more inch and it would have gone in off the post not ricocheted out.

Their left back, Andreas Brehme gave me a walloping on the back of me legs and I went down. But I didn't stay there. I stood up, went over to him and shook his hand. I wanted to show how real footballers act – not diving and play-acting. If I'd made a meal of the challenge, which he got booked for, it could have been a red. He'd have missed the final and who knows what would have happened. He scored the penalty that won it. But that is not what football should be about.

So the match went to penalties. I was on the list, and at one point I began to think what it would be like to take one. I imagined the buzz of scoring. But deep inside I knew my mind wasn't right. Peter Beardsley took mine I think.

As the gaffer was sorting everything out, he still found time to check I was alright. Incredible, really. He was telling us, 'Come on Paul, you've done yourself proud. I know you are going to miss the final but England can still get there. Just look at the crowd. See what it means to them. You are a massive part of that.' He was brilliant.

I was confident we would go through. We'd practised spot kicks but when it comes down to it, penalties are really just a fifty-fifty game. Peter scored, which was brilliant. So did Lineker before him and then Platty. It was 3–3 and next up was Stuart Pearce. It was brave of him to take one. I was watching from the centre circle and he hit it well, but the keeper got his legs to it. Bollocks. Stuart was crying. So was I.

They scored so it was down to Chris Waddle. Chris caught it sweet, but it kept rising and rising and it was all over. Funny thing was that when we got back to Luton, one of the guys on the plane had the actual ball. We'd been shooting towards the England end and he caught it. Good on Chris, he laughed when he heard. 'Bloody hell,' he said. 'I knew it was way over, but to reach Luton!'

'I didn't want it to end. I wanted to play football forever that summer.'

The team spirit that had been so strong throughout was there again. No one attached any blame to anyone. We were all in it together. We went there together and we came back together. When Chris missed, it was Terry Butcher who gave me a hug. That was nice of him. It showed how unselfish he was because he was hurting too.

Then I looked up and saw the crowd. I burst into tears again. They had come all that way to support us and they were still cheering. I was watching them thinking, how can I ever get back this time again? I knew I couldn't and I didn't want it to end. I wanted to play football forever that summer. Now it was all over.

Chris Waddle grabbed me by the arm. 'Come with me,' he said and took us in front of the roaring fans. 'They're for you, Paul.' Everything that had happened over the last six weeks hit me then. I was so grateful to Chris but more than that, I was grateful to the supporters for being there for us. My emotions were all over the place as Chris and I stood waving at the crowd.

In the dressing room I was still crying. So was Chris and a few others. Then we realised that Stuart Pearce wasn't there. After all that had happened, he had been pulled out of the hat for a random drugs test. He was away half an hour and we all felt for him – having to sit in a room with a German player, away from his team-mates.

The gaffer called us together. He was very emotional. 'You know, to me, you are winners. You have made me proud and you have made your country proud. Remember that forever and hold your heads high. You deserve to.' I called home and spoke to me dad, 'Good lad, son. You did well, today. You should be proud of yourself.' That made me feel a bit better.

Back at the hotel Bobby Robson said, 'Come on, I've got a present for you.' He had organised a party. He wanted to get our heads up and it sort of worked. We had a few beers and started to talk amongst ourselves about what a great time we'd had and how well we'd done. There has only ever been a handful of players who have made it to a World Cup semi-final. As I looked around, though, it struck me that this group would probably never be together again. There would be new faces, retirements. It was the end of this road.

FORE-TH!

The next morning I woke up and the buzz was gone. We went for a game of golf. It is not really my type of sport – I'm not good at taking one shot and then waiting twenty minutes for me next one – but it was a good distraction. Me, Chris, Steve McMahon and Dave Beasant played together. It was a fancy course, with strict etiquette. Not that you would have known it if you'd be following us. We got a buggy and were belting along. Chris was driving and I was hanging out the side with me top off, getting some sun. Chris deliberately drove

past a tree and a branch hit me in the chest, then whipped me on me arse. The gaffer saw us. 'Gascoigne! I can't believe you. Get your bloody shirt on. This is a top class course.' I was still getting a bollocking even though my World Cup was over.

We had to hang around waiting for the thrills of the third and fourth place play-off against Italy, which fortunately was only three days away. I didn't play in the match obviously, thanks to a certain Oscar-winning performance, but I still wanted to be part of it. Not being a sub I wasn't allowed on the bench, but that didn't stop me. I wanted to sit with the lads so I sneaked over in me flip-flops. We wanted to win, sure, but there was a sort of a party atmosphere as well. It was all about enjoying football and when the fans started a Mexican wave, we all joined in.

We were disappointed to lose the match, but it wasn't a big deal. To be honest, the third and fourth place medals were pretty much the same. That might sound a bit dismissive but it isn't meant to be. When they hung that World Cup medal around my neck it felt great. I kept staring at it, reading World Cup, World Cup over and over. Fourth place wasn't what we'd dreamed of, but it was still a hell of an achievement.

BACK HOME

We flew home before the final. I didn't know exactly what had been going on back in England. I had a rough idea I might get some attention, but for me it was really all about the whole squad, the whole England team, from the manager right through to the physios and the kit man. I'd loved every one of them and every bit of it. Even twenty-one years later, it makes me emotional thinking about Italia '90.

I did realise after the Germany game that blubbing on telly in front of millions might single me out, mind. But I could never have guessed what actually happened when I got home – people aged from three to ninety-three recognised us in the street. My world had changed forever.

'I probably shouldn't have eaten so many peanuts on the flight home.'

CHAPTER 7

TAYLOR MADE

ENGLAND:
SEPTEMBER 1990 –
SEPTEMBER 1993

Honestly Gaffer, I only drink
half shandies, and there's
this much lemonade.

After the World Cup, Bobby Robson did leave the England set-up, as had been widely discussed in the press prior to the tournament, to take up the manager's job with PSV Eindhoven. Then Graham Taylor arrived. I'd be lying if I said this was a particularly happy period for me and the national team, but that wasn't down to Taylor. Well, not all of it anyway.

I actually got on okay with Graham. He cared about the players and only wanted the best for them. The stick he got later, being called a turnip head and all that, I thought was totally out of order. His motives were good and although I didn't always agree with his style of play – he was more about going long or wide rather than through the middle – he got results and we qualified for the 1992 European Championships. Okay, that didn't go so well for England but there wasn't much I could do about that – I wasn't there. Thanks to me hernia, me knee and a broken leg I missed a load of games over these three years which is why this section is so short. The book's meant to be about me football highlights after all. Mmm. Next chapter please.

Hungary for a goal. Okay, okay I know. You don't need to tell us.

My first game under Taylor was in September 1990, in a friendly against Hungary and I also played in the Euro qualifier against Poland which we won 2–0 thanks to a Lineker penalty and a Peter Beardsley goal.

'I'd be lying if I said this was a particularly happy period for me and the national team'

Practice makes perfect. Over the next few years I got used to being carried off the pitch.

FORTY WINKS

Concentrating on the match? Concentrating on staying awake, more like.

In November 1990 I was dropped for the first time since I was a regular on the team, for the qualifier against Ireland. At least the manager had the balls to tell us face to face. He was good at the man-management stuff. We were doing a bit of loose training the day before the match and he pulled us out to give me the news. I tried to hold myself together and carry on working with the lads, but I didn't quite manage. I had a few tears and when I told the boys they couldn't believe it. Not about the tears, mind, they were used to that.

On the day of the game I bumped into Jack Charlton, who was still the Ireland boss. 'Take it easy today, eh lad', he said to me. 'I'm not playing.' 'What! Ah, that's great for us!' Then he invited me to his room for a Guinness. Why not, I thought. I hadn't slept much the night before, going over in me head what Graham Taylor had told us, so I needed a pick-me-up. I had a couple and then went down to the bench to watch the game.

Well, that's what I intended to do, but the lack of sleep and the Guinness got to me and I couldn't keep my eyes open. I fell asleep on Dave Seaman's shoulder. I'm not sure that really helped my case with Taylor but it didn't seem to do me any harm with the public. A month later I was voted BBC Sports Personality of the Year! I felt genuinely honoured having my name on that famous trophy alongside all the greats of British sport. I had never imagined something like that could happen to me. When I went up to accept the award I said that it was the best Christmas present I had ever had.

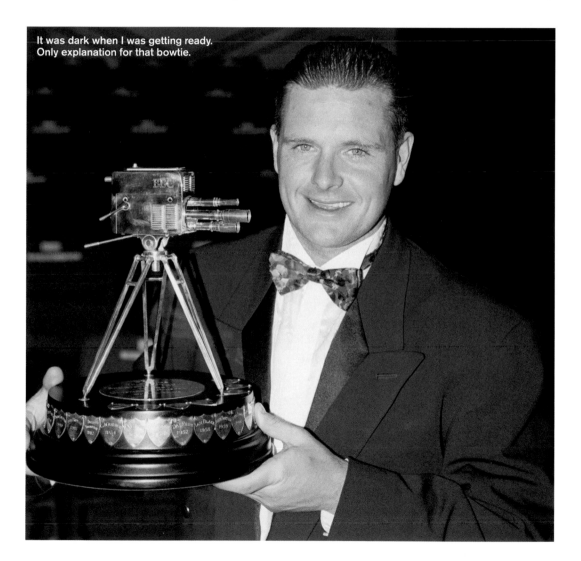

It was dark when I was getting ready. Only explanation for that bowtie.

NORWEGIAN BLUES

My first game back for England after my FA Cup final knee injury was against Norway at Wembley in October 1992. It was a World Cup qualifier. Phil Neal put us through the paces to make sure I was fully recovered. I felt good. I was excited to be back and decided to celebrate the fact two nights before the game with a couple of beers and a game of snooker with Paul Merson.

Paul was going through a hard time then, which I wasn't aware of, and throughout the evening he was knocking them back, brandy after brandy, all of which went on my room. I'd only had a handful of beers but when Taylor checked the bill the next day and saw the brandies he went mental. Paul is a mate and he had asked me not to tell anyone about the brandies, certainly not the gaffer, and I agreed to take the flack. So when Taylor called me in to say that me intake was 'disgusting', I kept quiet.

That was bad enough, but by then I had also managed to insult an entire nation. We were at the training camp and a Norwegian film crew were there. I was walking past when they asked me to say something to Norway. I tried to think of something funny and I came

up with a gem: 'Fuck off Norway.' I thought it was clear I was having a laugh, but they didn't take it that way. Lawrie McMenemy was the assistant manager at the time and he tried to defuse the situation, saying it was just a silly comment and hadn't meant any harm. I offered to give them a proper interview but the footage was still broadcast. Once again I was picking up negative press.

McMenemy was good to me. He was from Gateshead and I think he understood what I was like – more than some others, anyway. In the run-up to my return Taylor had sent him over to Italy, where I was now playing for Lazio, to see how I was doing at close hand. Poor Lawrie. I was on good behaviour, I wanted to get back into the England set-up, and anyway the training at Lazio was too brutal to mess around, but I led poor Lawrie astray. I had him drunk every night and I even took him to me sister's wedding where he was knocking it back and smoking cigars. Back in England when Taylor asked him if he had looked after me, I bet he replied, 'Yes, but Gazza didn't look after me!'

We drew the Norway match 1–1 and I played okay, although I was trying a bit too hard, a bit too intense, to let me football flow. You can see it here in me face.

Paul, did I buy these socks in Italy? What sort of state was I in?

RUNNING OUT OF FUEL

Next up was another qualifier: Turkey at Wembley on 18 November 1992. We won 4–0 and I scored twice – the only time I did that for England. The first one was a fairly straightforward shot inside the box that you can see at the beginning of the chapter, but it is the second one I remember best. It was one of me favourite goals, and one of the calmest I ever scored. The ball came across the box and I could have easy tapped it in but I waited for the keeper to commit himself and then just walked round him to slot it home. There are times in football when you know exactly what you are doing and you are in complete control. This was one of them for me, it felt fantastic.

By the following March our World Cup campaign was still on track. We went to Turkey in high spirits, having won two and drawn one, and performed well. In training Ian Wright and I were mucking about in the mud, giving everyone a laugh. The team enjoyed training together and we carried that spirit on to the pitch. The Turks must have been fed up with me by then because I scored against them again. I now began to believe that a second World Cup was a real possibility.

I thought at least I'd end up looking like Action Man with a scar across my cheek...

Then everything started to unravel. First, I got a smack in the face just before half-time in our next match against Holland at Wembley. I went up for a ball with Jan Wouters and his elbow's gone and cracked us across the cheek, fracturing it. We'd been two up but they got it back to 2–2 with a goal in the last five minutes. The result was a huge knock to our chances of qualification.

In June, the disappointment of the Holland result, which had been followed by a draw with Poland, was compounded in Oslo in what proved to be a disastrous few days.

Before the match, Taylor came out with a now infamous comment about my lifestyle. I don't know what prompted it – perhaps he was thinking back to the first Norway tie – but whatever it was he spoke to a press conference about my 'refuelling habits'. I honestly think he was trying to help me as he was getting increasingly worried about me drinking and eating, but all it did was create more negative headlines, which made things worse.

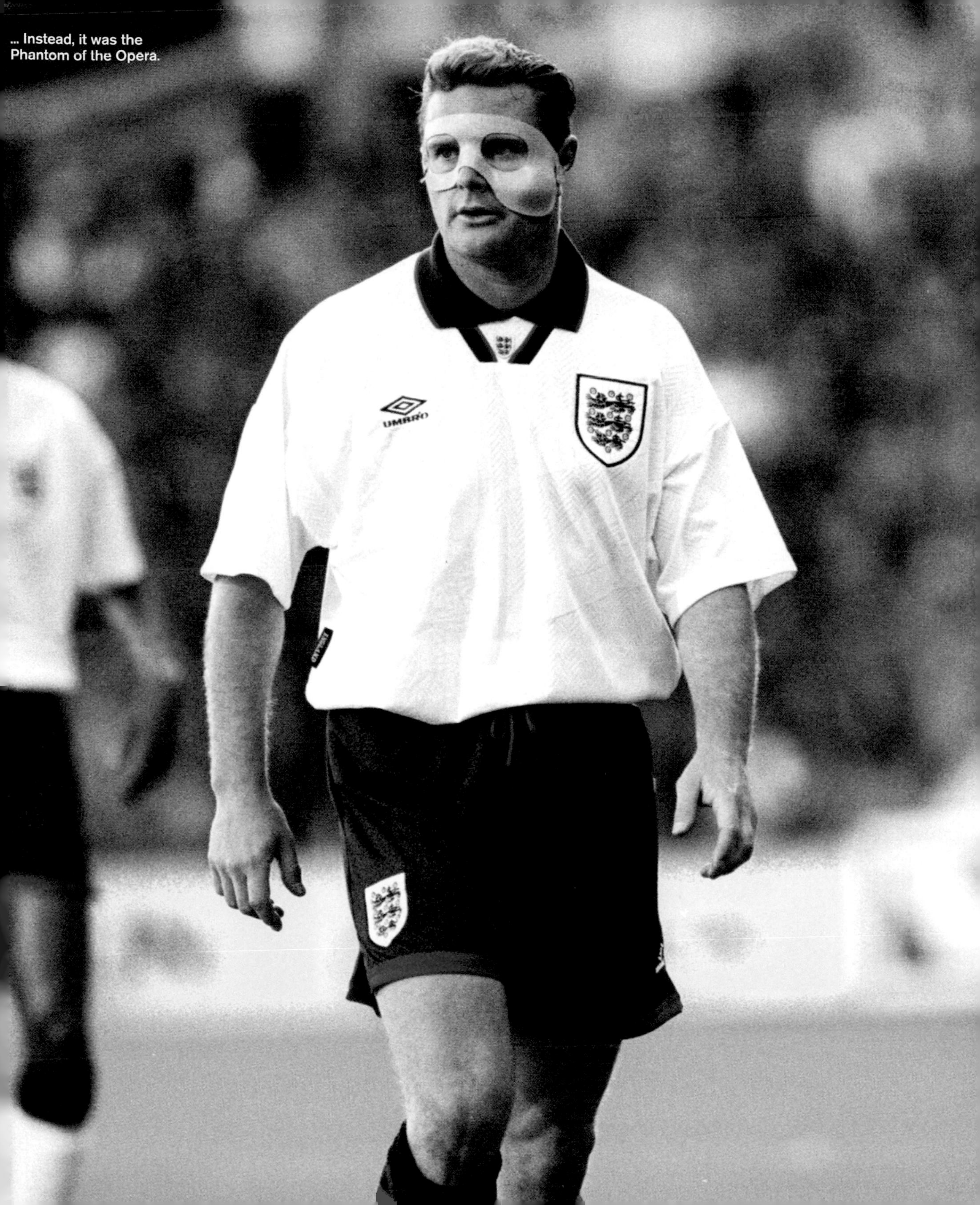

... Instead, it was the Phantom of the Opera.

In the Oslo game itself I tried hard to prove how good I was, attempting to take on the whole team and score, but they had set out to stop me and every time I touched the ball one or two of the Norwegians clattered into us. I couldn't get into any rhythm and neither could the team. At half-time we were one down and I lost it in the dressing room, shouting and swearing at everyone, saying Platty should get his fucking finger out because he was the captain; that our tactics were shit; all sorts. Lawrie McMenemy had to drag me into the toilet to get me to calm down. We ended up losing 2–0 which meant we had to win our last three qualifiers to be sure of making it to the World Cup. We did well in the match against Poland in September, winning 3–0. I scored the second – pictured here – and was pleased with my performance overall. The only downside was that I picked up a booking which ruled me out of the next match, against the Dutch in Rotterdam. England lost 2–0 which left us hoping for other results to go our way in the final round of matches. They didn't. England could look forward to a quiet summer and Graham Taylor, a new job.

Not that the failure to qualify ended up mattering to me. I wouldn't have been there anyway having broken me leg in April.

CHAPTER 8

ROMAN HOLIDAY

LAZIO:
MAY 1992 – JULY 1995

Ciao Signore Calleri. Je m'appelle Gazza.

nearly didn't make it to Lazio. And it wasn't because of me knee.

Gian Marco Calleri had bought the club with his brother Giorgio in the mid-80s. They'd both watched us during Italia '90 and Giorgio in particular was keen to sign me. Gian Marco, it seems, wasn't quite so sure. By early 1991, discussions between Spurs and Lazio were underway when in February, Giorgio very sadly died. This gave his brother a chance to pull out but the fans had got wind of the possible move and were adamant that they wanted me. So out of respect for his brother, Gian Marco went ahead with the deal. He was a lovely bloke, really friendly and good to me. Of course, then the whole move was delayed by a year, thanks to me knee, and so when I did eventually join Lazio, Gian Marco had sold the club to Sergio Cragnotti. I was lucky that he was also keen.

I first went over to Rome to formally meet the management and be introduced to the fans in August 1991, three months after the FA Cup final. I'd been working hard over that period, swimming, running, physio, so I was in good shape. When I arrived in Italy, the reception I received from the supporters was unbelievable, it was like being a movie star. They even made me a special banner, to make us feel welcome. I returned the compliment by saying a few words in Italian when I came out on to the Lazio pitch to wave at the fans. I think they liked that. Over my three years at the club I actually learned quite a lot of the language. I loved the city and the people so much that I wanted to make the most of me time there. I still remember some Italian – most of them swear words.

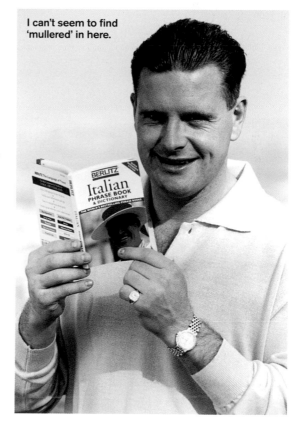

I can't seem to find 'mullered' in here.

So the August visit was a success and the deal was ready to be finalised when everything went pear-shaped again. I was on the receiving end of that punch in Newcastle a month later, so it was actually May 1992 before I formally became a Lazio player.

DINO ZOFF

The coach at Lazio at the time was Dino Zoff, the legendary Italian goalkeeper. I had a huge amount of respect for Zoff and got on well with him throughout my time in Italy. He obviously rated me because he gave me the number ten shirt. That's a huge honour over there. Some of the greatest players ever in the Italian league have worn the number ten, people like Roberto Baggio, Maradona and Michel Platini. I knew what wearing that shirt meant and I did my best not to let him or the club down, especially after he turned to me when he saw that banner the fans had put up and said, 'Paul, if you play well for me you can drink as much beer as you like.' That was just the sort of man-management I responded to.

These shorts are elasticated, right? Only kidding Dino. I won't drink that much beer.

CAPITAL CUP

Part of my transfer to Lazio from Spurs involved a
two-leg friendly between the two clubs. It was known
as the Capital Cup and the game in Italy in
September was my first real match since the FA Cup
final. I scored in the pouring rain and ran behind the
goal as I'd seen most of the Italians do when they
celebrated. I wanted to acknowledge the Lazio
supporters and make it clear I was now their man,
but equally I didn't want to go overboard. It didn't
feel right to do so.

   In the return leg the Spurs fans were brilliant, giving us a fantastic reception. Because of
the way the fans responded I actually really enjoyed the game although I had been a little
worried beforehand. I hoped I'd contributed enough to Spurs over the years and that the
supporters understood my reasons for leaving, but you never know how fans will react
when you leave a club. It did feel a little strange being back at White Hart Lane but as
soon as I heard the crowd and saw old friends I felt very much at home, like I'd never been
away. Gary Mabbutt probably thought that too, because from the kick off right through to
the final whistle I was taking the piss out of him, just like old times.

UP AND RUNNING

The games against Spurs were important to build up me match fitness, but the real business began on 27 September when I made me league debut for Lazio against Genoa. I lasted forty-five minutes. On the stroke of half-time I got a thump on me knee – me bad knee – and hit the deck hard. The whole stadium fell silent. I really thought that was going to be the end of my career. I gingerly got to me feet but for the final minute or so I did my best to avoid the ball. I didn't want to know what might happen if I made contact with it. Of course, I couldn't hide forever and eventually the ball came my way and I played a pass. My knee held up. It was the first time I really understood what an incredible job Mr Browett had done with his surgeon's knife. I was subbed at half-time as a precaution but sitting on the bench I made sure to let the fans know I was okay. It felt as though I had passed my first real test in Italy.

I was that upset I couldn't even work out which way round the shirt went.

So me opening game got off to a slightly stuttering start. But it was a lot better than me third, against AC Milan. They might not have been quite as unbelievable a side as when they won the European Cup twice on the trot, but they were still one hell of a team, Van Basten, Gullit, and Maldini amongst others. I knew it would be a good test of how Lazio were doing. The answer was clear. In comparison, we were rubbish. The 5–3 scoreline might suggest we were giving almost as good as we got, but the truth was they were all over us. I went mental in the changing room afterwards and had to be calmed down by Zoff. I was so desperate to do well that I over-reacted which wasn't the Italian way at all. I had a lot to learn.

DERBY DAY

Everyone said the Rome derby was different. I had played in derbies before and so I was like, 'Yeah, yeah, I know what to expect.' Fuck me, I was wrong. In the week running up to the match two or three thousand fans would turn up at training every day, chanting that we had to win. Then me team-mates started to say that if we lost we wouldn't be able to go out in the city for a month.

I had been warned to expect some pretty spectacular banners as the rival supporters tried to outdo each other. During the warm-up, I looked at the Roma end where all the fans were holding up either a red or blue card. Then they started spinning them. I'd never seen anything like it. The effect was like two giant Formula One cars racing each other, with the red for Roma in the lead obviously.

It was amazing. I couldn't imagine what our supporters could do to try and top that, but they did. Out of nowhere there was suddenly a gigantic Lazio shirt being held up. It was so massive it virtually covered the entire end of the stadium! What a way to start the match.

Back in the changing room the president came in and announced that we would each receive the equivalent of £3,000 in cash if we won; half of that if it was a draw. It was more than the normal bonus but I reckoned he could do better than that. 'Hold on, this is the derby! What about £5,000 for a win and £2,500 for a draw?' I used me translator for that bit – I didn't want to mess up the numbers and end up asking for less. The president must have admired me balls for trying it on because he agreed to pay the extra money.

I played okay, but nothing more. They were one up with only minutes to go when we got a free kick. Beppe Signori went up to take it and I said to him, 'Beppe, leave it and get in the box. You're a striker.'

'No, no. You go, Paul. I can't head it, I'm tiny.'

'Well, I can't fucking head it either! I'm useless. You get in and I'll whip it across.' He was having none of it though so eventually, with time running out, I left it to him. The ball came over, a little behind us, but I threw meself at it, put a strong neck on it and made good contact. It was another slow-motion moment. I thought for a second the keeper was going to get there but he seemed to just watch it go in. It was too good for him I guess...

When it hit the back of the net, the first thought that came to us was that at least I'd be able to leave the house. That Rome derby really was like life or death, and with three minutes to go we'd managed to stay alive. It had taken eighteen months but at last I felt I'd finally arrived at Lazio. Oh, and we got our cash plus I was given a bit extra – a crate of Newcastle Brown. Goes lovely with pasta.

THE FANS

I was pleased with how that first season at Lazio went. I played twenty-two league games and scored four goals. Not bad, considering I'd been out of football for so long. The Italian press never seemed to take to us though, probably because I did daft things like burping into a mike live on telly before a match – not a popular move in Italy. But the fans were brilliant, which was really all that mattered because in Italy the fans come first.

For our pre-season training camp they would turn up in their hundreds and we'd let them in to watch the sessions. You couldn't have stopped them even if you had wanted to – they would have just ended up ripping the place apart to get to the team. I liked being that close to the supporters. It was one of the things that made my time in Italy so special. When they produced these huge banners with me name on them, it actually made me feel quite humble. I was surprised that they had gone to all that bother for me. And I am sure that pouring water over someone is a traditional way of showing affection in Italy...

ITALIAN BREAK

My second season at Lazio went okay too. I suffered from a few tweaks and niggles but nothing serious and up until April 1994, I'd played seventeen games and scored a couple of goals. I'd even taken the captain's armband for one match, which was a great honour. It couldn't last…

We'd played on the Sunday and normally we'd have the next day off, but for some reason we were called in for training. I wasn't too impressed. We were having a five-a-side kick around, and at one point I let one of their players get past me and he scored. My team went mad. Zoff went mad. Then I went mad. 'Alright, if you want fucking serious football, you'll get fucking serious football.'

Two seconds later, the ball came between me and Alessandro Nesta, who was only a kid back then. I went in hard on him, but missed the ball and kicked his calf. Snap. Actually – snap, snap. It was totally my fault and I knew I'd broken me leg the moment it happened. Turns out it was me fibula and tibia. The lads helped carry me off the training pitch but they weren't walking in time and kept jarring me and bumping me leg. It was agony. I eventually got to hospital where they gave me morphine and said they were going to operate in the morning.

Later that evening our captain, Claudio Sclosa, came to see me. Claudio and I used to

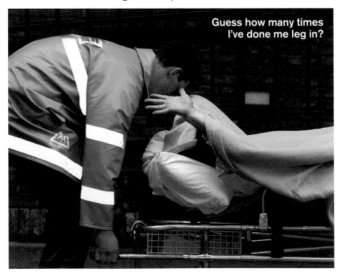

Guess how many times I've done me leg in?

room together – which he loved, obviously, especially when I used to watch telly, talk on me phone and play Nintendo all night long. Claudio said to me, 'Look Paul, hospitals are different here to what you are used to at home. You should go back to London. To the same surgeon. I'll sort out a flight for you.' Top bloke that Claudio.

So that's what I did. Back to the Princess Grace Hospital

and Mr Browett. When I looked at the X-ray after the operation he had mended the tibia but the fibula was still in bits. I asked why that was and he said it would heal itself. It did, eventually, but first he had to insert a steel rod into the marrow. Ouch. When the time came to take it out I tried to persuade him to leave it there. I reckoned I could make some hefty challenges with that as support, but he was having none of it. Spoilsport.

ARRIVEDERCI

As I was recovering from me broken leg, Dino Zoff moved upstairs at Lazio to become president and we had a new manager, Zdenek Zeman. He was Czech and tough as hell. When I told him I was back and ready to play he said, 'No. You are overweight. I call you Fatty. You are unfit.' He told me I had to lose two stone before he'd even think about picking us, so I didn't have much choice but to buckle down as best I could. It was murder. He was a good manager, but at times I thought he was the devil.

Before the start of the new season, we were training in Switzerland and Zeman said to me one day that I wasn't to join the lads but instead I had to work out in a local gym on me own. It was a couple of miles away so I cycled there. Next thing I know, one of the coaches arrives and he tells me that I have to take the bike back and then run to the gym. I was furious! I went to the training ground where the lads were, stood on the top of the steps and threw down five mountain bikes that Zeman had just bought to help with the training. 'You want your fucking bikes, here they are.' That showed him. I had to buy new ones of course...couldn't have the lads pissed off at me.

'When I told him I was back and ready to play he said, 'No. You are overweight. I call you Fatty.'

Zeman had been a basketball coach in Sicily previously. I remember once the Lazio fans were giving him a hard time when we were going through a bad patch. 'Fucking hell, Boss, have you ever heard anything like that before?'

'Much worse. When I was manager in Sicily, we weren't doing well and an angry fan came into the dressing room and put a gun against my head. He said he would shoot me if we lost the next match.'

'What happened? Did you lose the next game?'

'Do you think I stayed around to risk it? So these fans, they don't bother me.'

Eventually, I did get fit but he didn't play us much. In fact, I only played four more times for the club. Zeman and me were getting on fine by then, but I just don't think my style fitted into his plans. Then all these rumours started to fly around that Lazio were looking to sell us. I wasn't happy that no one was speaking to me about it, so I went to see Zoff. I burst into his office and said, 'What the hell's going on? You trying to get rid of us on the sly?'

'No, no. It is not like that. Yes, I have been speaking to some clubs, but nothing is confirmed yet. That's why I haven't mentioned it. I can let you know who might be interested.'

I had too much respect for him to stay angry for long. 'Okay, that's fine. Thanks.'

'The first one is Chelsea. Do you want to meet them?'

'Alright.'

'Aston Villa?'

'Alright.'

'Rangers?'

'No chance. I am not signing for them.'

I went home and called Bryan Robson to ask him if he would have a word with Alex Ferguson, to see if he was still interested. 'Why don't you ask him yourself, he is sitting right next to me.' I spoke to Fergie and said that I knew I had let him down before but asked if he would consider me again. He said he was interested but he was waiting to see how things developed with Cantona. 'If he leaves, we'll see.' Deep down I could tell he wasn't going to sign us, so I had to let that one go.

I met with Glenn Hoddle, then Chelsea manager, over lunch but I had a loose tooth that day and lost it in the sandwich I was eating. I was more interested in looking for that than in what he had to say so that was never likely to work out. I also met Doug Ellis from Villa who explained all about the great stuff he had at the club but I got the feeling he wanted me more as a name than for my football.

I went back to Zoff and told him I wasn't interested in Villa or Chelsea. 'I understand Paul. That's fine. But I am surprised you didn't want to look more closely at Rangers.'

'I am just not that interested in QPR.'

'Not Queens Park Rangers! Glasgow Rangers.'

'Why didn't you say that! Get them on the phone.' I had met Walter Smith a few years previously in Florida and I remembered thinking then that I would like to play for him, so this was much more interesting to me. Walter came to meet us in Italy soon after and it all

I used subtle
tactics to
persuade
Zeman to sell
me to Rangers.

happened quite quickly from there. We got on; I spoke to the chairman David Murray, liked what he had to say, and that, as far as I was concerned, was that. I left it to my advisers and Rangers to sort out the detail and went off on holiday. By the time I was due back, however, it was all still dragging on. My guys were trying to get the best deal possible but I just wanted it settled. 'Listen, I don't care if it is a drop in wages. Take the deal.'

They made the call to Walter and it was done. I asked me mate Jimmy to sort out everything in Italy – the villa, cars and all that – while I flew straight to Glasgow and never looked back.

CHAPTER 9

BACK ON TRACK

RANGERS:
JULY 1995 – JUNE 1996

had never been in a dressing room like it in me life before. Being with the Spurs lads was fantastic but at Rangers it was something different; they were all loopy. Most of them, anyway. Richard Gough was fairly normal. From day one the other players took the piss out of us and I knew immediately I would fit in. It was like that the whole time I was there. A real one-for-all-and-all-for-one mentality. We might have the odd squabble in training but on the pitch we were tight, always supporting each other. I loved it.

As always, my timing was perfect. I was just back from holiday when I started at the club and I arrived to meet the fans in the sunshine, looking tanned and healthy. I also had a new hairdo. Pretty soon they were all copying me – either that or the Scottish sun had bleached everyone's hair. I think it's more likely I set a trend.

From the moment I arrived at Ibrox, all I wanted to do was start playing. I had the buzz back that had been missing throughout that last year at Lazio. The fans in Italy had been good to me but with all the injuries I don't think I showed my real potential. I saw Rangers as an opportunity to enjoy football again and I was desperate to get cracking.

Two of the reasons I wanted to join the club were the manager, Walter Smith, and his assistant, Archie Knox. They had both won so much in their careers and I wanted to be part of their success. The trophy cabinet was scary – and that was only the silverware they had on display. There was another massive pile packed away somewhere. There was a constant pressure to maintain that level of achievement which some people might have found intimidating, but I liked it. Up to then I had only won one senior trophy – and big shock, I was in hospital for that one. I was desperate for more.

I trained hard at Rangers. You had to – Walter and Archie expected to win every game three or four nil. If we weren't up at half-time we got a bollocking. I loved the style of the training we did – it was all about the ball. For specific games, perhaps the Champions League or a difficult cup tie, we would work on set pieces, but in the main we just played football. Scots versus Europeans. Everyone got wired in, and that gave us a fantastic competitive edge in matches.

If we mucked around too much during the sessions, Archie would go mental. He would call us in for extra training and give us a hammering. Other times he would surprise us. If we beat Celtic, for instance, the next day Archie might say, 'Right, get your trainers on.' I used to think it meant we were going for a run, but no. He would take us to an ice cream parlour and then for a walk near Celtic Park with 99s in our hands. What a laugh.

One of the things that struck me early on at Rangers was the passion of the fans. Sure, at Ibrox I expected the noise and the atmosphere to be incredible, but even when we were away it felt as though we were playing at home. The fans travelled everywhere and it gave us a huge boost wherever we walked out on to the pitch.

David Murray was another reason I was so happy at Rangers. He is an amazing man, a really nice guy and a fantastic chairman. He's been on crutches for so many years, having lost both legs in a car crash back in the 70s, but you wouldn't know it. If you ever tried to open the door for him he'd go off on one. He was tough but incredibly decent and fair. From the very start he made sure I had somewhere comfortable to live and he would come round and take me out, just to make sure I was okay and not lonely. Way beyond what a chairman normally does and I was grateful.

It's hard being a style icon.

Tradition was important at Rangers. When David Murray first showed me around the stadium, he explained the history of the place and the role the club played in the community. 'Respect for Rangers Football Club is critical,' he said. 'That's why you are expected to always wear a suit and tie when you turn up for training.' I was pretty sure he hadn't seen some of me outfits, but I understood his point and I was happy to follow the rules.

Some traditions can be a bit scary, though, when you aren't expecting them. In one of me early matches we got a throw in and I went to take it. Just as I picked up the ball I noticed a small plaque in the grass with someone's name on it and 'RIP'. I looked along and there were loads of them. I got the fright of me life, dropped the ball and ran on to the pitch shouting, 'Someone else take it!' Later it was explained to me what they were about and I realised those plaques were special. They marked where the ashes of some fans had been scattered and showed the deep connection between the club and the supporters.

CARELESS WHISTLE

Winding each other up was an important part of the bonding at Rangers. It was all good-natured and most of it didn't make the press. But some of it did – big time. We were playing Steaua Bucharest in a pre-season tournament, just after I'd signed, and I scored my first ever Rangers goal. As you can imagine, I was excited. Before the match one of the lads had told me that if I did knock one in, the best way to get the fans on my side was to pretend to play the flute in celebration. I honestly had no idea what the implications of this were in Glasgow; how it was a reference to the Orange Lodge marches and that it would antagonise Celtic supporters.

I did the next morning though, when the photos appeared in the papers. I was mullered for my insensitivity. It didn't matter that I was totally innocent. It was a big deal for a day or so, but it calmed down. You would have thought it was enough to have taught me a lesson. Me? A lesson? Come on.

Honestly, there were some fans there. And unfortunately some photographers as well...

FIRSTS

Firsts play a big part whenever you join a new club. The press and supporters are always on the lookout for them and they can take on an unnatural significance, which can be distracting. So you want to chalk them off as quickly as you can and move on. Of course some 'firsts' are great, and at Rangers I had more than me fair share of those, like me first league and cup double and me first Players' Player of the Year award. But alongside these are always the less than glorious ones, such as me first bit of aggro with a team-mate on the pitch. Here I've picked out a few which make me smile.

FIRST OLD FIRM GOAL

I maintained an interesting record at Rangers. Well I think it's interesting at least. Since leaving Newcastle I scored me first league goal for each new club in local derbies, against Arsenal, Roma and now Celtic. It was my second Old Firm match, but my first in the league. Ally McCoist had the ball out on the right and he whipped over a big, bending cross. I saw the keeper come for it but I knew I

Excited? Just a bit.

was going to get there first so all I had to do was make a decent contact and steer it past him. I got my foot to it and it was job done and dusted. What a feeling! I was already aware what a massive deal these games were and to score against the arch rivals on their home turf – just brilliant.

After I knocked it in I ran to the Rangers end to celebrate. I was shouting and screaming me head off when I noticed a big, mean-looking, baldy Celtic fan in the next section. He was pointing and swearing, looking like he wanted to kill us. So being the nice, sensitive bloke that I am I turned towards him and gave it everything I had. I made sure I was out of reach, mind – I'm not that daft.

FIRST SCOTTISH CAP

Early on in my time at Rangers I decided to get me teeth done so that I would look even better when I was holding all those trophies at the end of the season. It took loads of visits to the dentist to get them sorted and at one stage I was fitted with temporary caps. They were massive, sticking out a mile. I knew I was in trouble when the next day me dad, who was up visiting, waved us off on me way to training with the parting shot, 'Good luck, son.'

When I arrived at the ground the first person I saw was the receptionist. I asked her if she could notice anything different

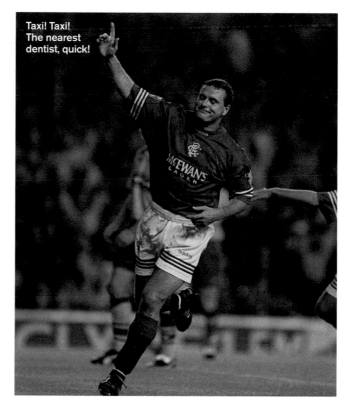

Taxi! Taxi! The nearest dentist, quick!

about me. She stared, open mouthed. 'What the hell have you done to your teeth!'

I didn't want to go into the dressing room. It was a cert I'd get nailed. But I had no choice so I decided to try and keep me mouth shut. The first person I saw was Ally McCoist. 'Morning Gazza.' I nodded at him. 'Mmmmm.' I was trying not to smile but I couldn't manage it and Coisty started laughing his head off. 'Don't say anything to the lads,' I pleaded. Fat chance. As soon as everyone arrived, Ally called out, 'Come on Gaz, show the boys.' I stood in the middle of the dressing room and gave them a big grin, at which point Coisty pipes up, 'Gazza, you could eat an apple through a letter box with them.' I cracked up.

We were playing Motherwell on the Saturday and I knew I'd be in for a roasting if anyone noticed…which naturally they did. I scored in the match and as you can see in the photo, I did my best to stay tight-lipped. But I was never very good at that on the pitch and the next day I got hammered in the papers. No one mentioned my goal, just the state of me gob. I was gutted.

FIRST GOAL OF THE SEASON AWARD

It was the evening of Thursday, 28 December 1995. I was at home relaxing when Walter Smith called. 'Paul, what are you doing?'

'Nothing. Why?'

'Get ready. You're coming out with me and Archie. We'll pick you up in five minutes.'

I didn't want to go but I couldn't exactly say no. Five minutes later they were at the door, buzzing like crazy and beeping the horn. They took me to a nice restaurant where we had about six bottles of white wine. I think Walter and Archie must have heard stories about my drinking and wanted to see for themselves if I could keep it under control. It was like they were testing me. And I am pretty sure I failed.

By the end of the meal I was pretty hammered but I thought I'd just about got away with it, especially when Archie said, 'Right Gaz, no more white wine for you.' That was a relief, but then he continued, 'Here's a bottle of red.' That was the one that finished us off. By the time they dropped me at home I was out of it so I had no idea what Walter meant when he called from the car, 'Gaz, you better score a brace on Saturday.' What have me teeth got to do with anything, I thought as I staggered through the front door. It wasn't until I asked someone at training the next day that I realised he meant two goals.

We were playing Hibs on the Saturday. We won 7–0 and I scored what was later voted the goal of the season. I dribbled right through the whole defence before cracking it home. I thought surely that would make up for the state I'd got meself into at the restaurant. No chance. I got a bollocking in the changing room after for not doing what I was told and only scoring the one.

FIRST TIME BOOKING A REF

This happened in the same match as the goal of the season. I was making a dart through the Hibs defence but I overran the ball and it went out of play. As I turned round I notice the ref's yellow card lying on the grass. I picked it up and ran over to him, pretending to book him for a laugh before handing it back. He didn't see the funny side. He took it off me and said, 'And here's one for you as well.' The whole ground went mental. The fans were booing and whistling and even the Hibs players got involved saying things like, 'What the hell are you doing? That's not fair, it's just because it is Paul Gascoigne.' I appreciated them backing me up but the booking stood.

FIRST TIME HURDLING

We were playing Partick Thistle at Firhill in early February 1996. In the papers that morning I'd read a report that one of their players, Billy McDonald, had said he was going to get the better of us, that I was overweight and he was going to make sure I didn't score. I have no idea if he actually said any of that stuff but in the tunnel I looked across at him and said 'Alright mate. I saw the papers this morning. Welcome to your worst nightmare.'

The two of us were niggling at each other throughout the match. I don't think it helped matters much when he lost the ball in the midfield and I burst through their defence to score the opener. In celebration I hurdled the hoardings and mimed a big 'I'm so fat' gesture. It amused me but I did get booked for leaving the field of play.

I must have been getting fat right enough. I needed help to get back on the pitch.

Billy McDonald, in the middle here, about to start our wrestling bout.

Thistle equalised not long afterwards with a belter, but it wasn't quite as good as my winner which I curled in from outside the box minutes later. In the second half the niggling turned to wrestling as McDonald and I clashed again. It is fair to say tempers were now frayed. Towards the end of the match I was making a run, shielding the ball, with McDonald nipping at me heels trying to get around us. I held him off and he took a bit of a knock. That was probably the last straw. A few seconds later I had the ball near the corner and saw him charging towards me. I know what it is like…he was upset about what he thought was a foul and he lost the plot for a moment. I nutmegged him and that was it. He took a wild swipe with his right boot, missed us and was sent off. Bit of a nightmare, right enough.

He was a good young lad though, Billy McDonald, a decent player and there was no problem between us afterwards. In fact, I signed me boots and gave them to him as a present. 'When you are good enough to fit into them, put them on.' We laughed about it and he later apologised in the papers for what had happened.

CHAMPIONEES!
CHAMPIONEES!

Sunday, 28 April 1996: Rangers versus Aberdeen in the second last game of our season. Just thinking about this match now brings tears to my eyes, although I know that's not saying a lot. We needed a win to clinch the Scottish Championship, Rangers' eighth in a row. The only trouble was that after nineteen minutes, we were one down.

Not long after, we won a corner on the left. Brian Laudrup played it to me at the edge of the box. It was one of those moments when I could see what was on without consciously thinking about it. I dummied with my right, cut inside the box, and managed to get me boot round the ball to crash it into the roof of the net just as a last-ditch challenge came in.

Over the next hour or so of the match I was fairly quiet. For some reason the goal had drained me of energy and I was struggling with the pace of the game. With about ten minutes to go Alan McLaren turned to me and said, 'Come on, Paul, we need something.' 'I can't, Alan,' I told him. 'I've got nothing left.' Just then the ball broke to me, midway inside our half, and a hole opened up in front of us. Come on, Paul, give it a go, I thought. So I did, fending off defenders with my arms while others dropped away, until I made it into the box and curled it home with my left this time.

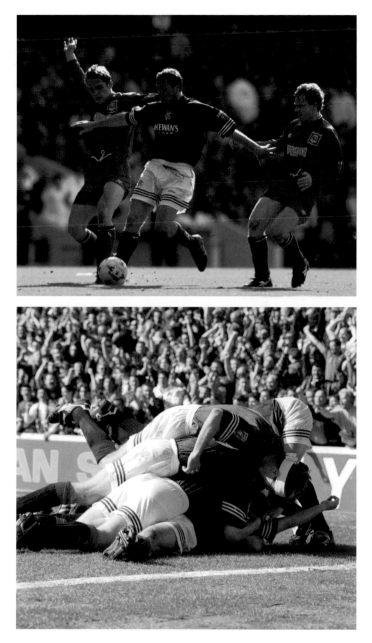

I find it hard to describe the feeling at that moment. The noise of the fans was incredible. It meant so much to all those people in the stadium, to Walter and Archie and all the players. I was almost delirious I think. I certainly was, after about eight of my team-mates jumped on us as I lay on the grass screaming me head off. If Alan McLaren had decided to join the pile-up I think that might have been the end of my days. Wouldn't have been a bad way to go, I suppose.

Five minutes later, Gordon Durie made a run on the right and was brought down. Penalty. Coisty normally took them but the thought of scoring my first hat trick for Rangers in the match that brought the Championship, in front of the home supporters, was too much for me. I gave it everything I had, laying it on with a trowel. Big, wide eyes, tears welling, a croak in me voice, begging him for the ball, telling him how much it would mean to me. He tried to claim there was a chance he would be leaving the club and this might be his last ever goal for the team he loved. I wasn't having it. 'If you're leaving, what does it matter?' I said. 'I'm staying, so I should take it.' Coisty didn't leave that summer, thank God, but he did toss me the ball. 'Go on, Gaz. It's your game.' Thanks, Ally.

When that ball nestled in the corner of the net I knew we were champions.

There are two moments that stick in my mind from the mayhem of the celebrations that followed. The first involved Ian Durrant in a moment of such quality it sums up the man.

In many respects, when I arrived

at Rangers I was Durranty's replacement. The team had an incredibly strong spine at that time, with Andy Goram and Richard Gough at the back, Alan McLaren and Stuart McCall doing the nasty, hard work in the middle and Coisty up front. What they were looking for was a spark of creativity, which had been Durranty. It still was, to some extent, because he still had that crackerjack football brain, but he was never quite the same following that terrible knee injury he suffered back in 1988 which kept him out for two-and-a-half years.

I like to think that if a replacement was necessary, Ian was pleased it was me. He certainly never resented my appearance at the club or created any feeling of awkwardness – the opposite in fact. He was always joking with me, making me feel welcome and part of the team.

Even still, it must have been hard for Durranty that Sunday afternoon. He wasn't in the starting line-up but he came on at the end and it was him who went and got the hat-trick ball for me. I thought that was an amazing gesture. It was an incredibly generous thing to do – a lesser person would probably have been sulking. Not him. He threw me the ball and told me to get up on his shoulders. Pure class. I had a lot of laughs with Ian. I stayed overnight at his house once after we'd been out for a few beers. We were a bit pissed when we got back and I was worried about sleeping in as I knew if I was late for training I'd get a right bollocking. Durranty didn't need to be in first thing so I said to him that somehow he had to make sure I was up in time. 'No problem. I've put an alarm clock in your room.' What I didn't know was that while I was asleep he put the clock forward by two hours. So when I thought it was nine in the morning, it was only seven. The alarm went off and I jumped up, called a taxi and shot off to the ground. I thought it was a bit quiet on the roads but didn't suss what had happened. When I got there everything was still locked up. And it was freezing. I had to hang around like a right prat until the ground staff turned up. Durranty was good like that – always coming up with something clever.

The other thing that winning the Championship reminds me of is sitting in the hotel bar having a drink with pretty-boy Davie Dodds from the coaching staff. We'd all been going crazy celebrating in the dressing room directly after the game, but this was some time later. We were having a really good time, quiet but happy, when all of a sudden a couple of bottles of champagne arrived at the table. I turned round to see who had sent them and it was the Aberdeen players, who were staying overnight there. They came over and congratulated us on our win and stayed for a drink. That was really nice of them – especially as they ended up buying us about eleven bottles. Cheers lads.

THE DOUBLE

We completed the league and cup double on 18 May 1996 with a 5–1 demolition of Hearts. Gordon Durie and Brian Laudrup quite rightly took all the plaudits that afternoon, with Gordon bagging a hat trick and Brian a brace. (See, I'm learning.) In fact, I think they set up each other's goals as well. So it was pretty much a two-man show.

But to me, the real hero was John Brown, our fullback. John was Rangers mad. He loved the club and was desperate to play every match. In the cup final that day his Achilles went with about twenty minutes to go. He must have been in agony; still he played on. I don't know how he did it but it showed how much the club meant to him. He wanted to be there at the end, when the ref blew the final whistle. That really got to me. I thought he was incredibly brave.

I didn't play brilliantly in the game but it didn't matter, with Brian and Gordon in such sensational form. The work rate Gordon put in wasn't natural for a centre forward. He was everywhere on the park that day. I used to wind Gordon up, telling him he didn't score enough goals, so I was really pleased for him when his hat-trick proved what a great striker he really was.

Brian Laudrup was an amazing player. In training, even if you knew exactly what Brian was about to do, you still couldn't stop him. I remember Stuart McCall trying to get the ball off him eight or nine times and he couldn't get near it, when all Brian was doing was the same trick each time.

Me and Brian used to have a right laugh on the pitch. If we were 2–0 up, say, we would pass the ball to each other, around the opposition, and I'd go 'Waheey,' and he'd go 'Waheey, upalay, upalay.' It used to drive the other team mad.

If we needed a break in a game for whatever reason then we would give the ball to Brian and ask him to keep a hold of it for five minutes. And he would. He was fast and would take on players for fun. But he was never selfish. Peter Beardsley was like that too, both of them setting up as many goals as they scored themselves.

FISHY TALE

Thinking about that Scottish Cup win and Gordon Durie reminds me of fish.

The photo opposite is from a fishing trip we all went on in Denmark, during a pre-season tour. Me and Durranty decided to race two crabs that we had caught, with money riding on the outcome. We marked the finish line and then held our crabs in position while someone called out, 'Ready, steady, go!' We let go at the same time. My crab shot off to the left, Durranty's to the right. We'd forgotten, crabs walk sideways…

Anyway, back to Gordon Durie. As I mentioned earlier, there was a lot of banter and mickey-taking in the Rangers dressing room. We were always looking to get one over on each other and at some point Gordon had stitched me up like a kipper (see, fish again) over something. I can't remember exactly what it was, but I was definitely out for a spot of revenge. I didn't rush into it though. I bided me time until the exactly the right moment and then I hooked him good and proper. Alright, I know, enough with the fish references.

I asked to borrow his car after training one day. I told him I needed to shoot off to pick something up but that I'd be back in ten minutes. 'No bother,' he said. 'Take your time!' I'd been fishing early that morning, as I often did before training, and I had a couple of trout with me which were part of me plan. I drove the car down the road a bit and then pulled over, out of sight. I put one of the trout in the boot, so it could be found easily. I knew that's

where he would look once the smell started. But I also squeezed the second one in between the back seat and the floor of the car, well hidden.

A couple of days later Durie came up to us. He'd obviously smelt the fish. 'Ah Gazza, you're not smart enough to get me.' And he handed me the trout from the boot. 'Good try, mate.' Three or four days after he came up to us again: 'My car still stinks. I can't understand it.' I told him it was probably just the smell taking time to clear.

Ian Ferguson then borrowed Gordon's car. It was a hot day and he had the windows down. When he came back he said, 'It's weird. When I was driving it was fine, but every time I stopped at traffic lights, I could smell rotting fish.' That cracked me up, but I didn't say anything. Eventually Gordon had to take the car to a valeting service. While they were cleaning it one of the guys spotted the fish tail sticking out. When he found out, Gordon went mental, but it was worth it. The rest of the lads were very impressed when I told them what I had done, saying I was a genius for coming up with the two-fish plan. The chairman wasn't too chuffed though. The car was a sponsored one, provided by the club. I think it had to be scrapped eventually.

CHAPTER 10

FOOTBALL'S COMING HOME

EURO '96: GROUP STAGE

When Terry Venables was announced as the England manager in 1994, let's just say I was happy. Graham Taylor and me, well, we got on but we hadn't been a total love match as I've said – unlike me and the new gaffer. When Terry was given the job he made a point of meeting all the players in person. I was at Lazio at the time so we met at the Cavalieri Hilton in Rome on Valentine's Day. I didn't know he liked me that much.

I'd obviously worked with Terry at Spurs so when he became the new boss, before the first training session, some of the lads asked me what he was like. All I could say was, 'I don't know how to explain it. Come to me at the end of the week and you tell me what you think.' A week later I remember the lads saying, 'Paul, he's unbelievable to work for. I would love him to be me club manager.' Terry was one of the key reasons I went to Spurs in the first place, with all due respect for Sir Alex. He guided me and looked after me – and gave me bollockings when I needed them. But he never embarrassed me in the dressing room. He knew that would upset me. He was smart like that. Instead he'd pull me to one side and ask me to come to his office. His style wasn't hairdryers, he never swore – well once he called us shit after a match against Sunderland – but what he said always got through to me.

That's Amore...

TRIP TO THE DENTIST

Ahead of the Euro '96 tournament Terry Venables took the squad away to China and Hong Kong. In Beijing we had a day off and a load of the lads went on a trip to the Great Wall. I couldn't be bothered, it was too far so I was happy to sit about, in the Jacuzzi mostly. When the lads got back they were pissed off because they didn't get to see much of the wall because there was repair work being done and the

steps to the top were blocked off. It is old, I suppose…

The whole trip was seen by some afterwards as a misguided giant piss-up, but that was total rubbish. We trained hard, played two matches and it was only right at the end that we let our hair down, which is important for team spirit.

For the match against China in Beijing the noise inside the Workers' Stadium was astonishing. Perhaps it was because of the goal I scored. It was one of those I had always dreamed about. I was through on goal and as the keeper came out to meet me he spread himself big but I threw him a dummy and casually flicked the ball over him without looking. I got Man of the Match which all the guys said was the right choice, especially because I had this Chinese guy all over me like a rash. He clearly only had one job to do on the pitch, which was to try and stop me. Hard luck, mate.

Mystery injury? Nah. Blister? Nah. I didn't play because me eye was gummed up.

From China we went to Hong Kong. I didn't play in the game against the Hong Kong XI and there was press speculation that I had a mystery injury. Terry told the press it was because I had a blister following the game against China but I can now exclusively reveal the truth: as you can see here, me eye was gummed up.

After the match Terry Venables told us we could go for a night out. It was me birthday the next day so we all decided to celebrate. We went to a sort of theme bar, but it was all a bit quiet and boring until I overheard Robbie Fowler. He was talking to a girl at the bar. 'Hi, I'm Robbie Fowler' he said. 'I'm a footballer.' It cracked me up. I told him it was the worst chat-up line ever. That broke the ice and we started to muck around. Steve McManaman got involved, saying to Robbie, 'Here's a present for you,' and – boof – poured a glass of beer over his head. I was next to get one, then Teddy Sheringham. After that, anyone from the team who walked in was greeted with a 'Hiya' and a pint. Alan Shearer was priceless. He saw what was happening, and said, 'Hi guys, I'll save you the bother' and poured a pint over his own head.

We then moved on to some weird cocktails called Flaming Lamborghinis. We got wired into them and for no reason I can remember, the next game was to rip each other's shirts off. It was all a right laugh, just a bunch of guys letting their hair down. I was getting a bit tired though, so I decided to slip off for a rest in a telephone booth. It was that sort of bar. Don't ask me what the theme was. So I was having a doze when suddenly the door of the booth flew open and there stood Dennis Wise and Teddy Sheringham. They each had a boxing glove on, which they had found on the wall behind the bar. They must have been made in the year zero, they were that heavy. So Teddy gave us one in the ribs and as I bent over, Dennis cracked me with an upper cut. I was wide awake after that.

Someone then suggested we give the dentist's chair a go. What you had to do was lie back in the seat while the barman poured various spirits down your neck. It seemed like the best idea ever and about eight of us had a go. What we didn't know was that someone in the bar had taken photos. Thanks pal. They appeared in the British papers afterwards and of course who got all the blame?

'What we didn't know was that someone in the bar had taken photos. Thanks pal.'

Not long afterwards, Bryan Robson appeared. He wasn't playing, he was one of the coaches by then, but that didn't stop me ripping off his new shirt. Everything just came away except the collar. He looked so funny – like a Chippendale. I thought for a second he might be annoyed but he took it all in really good spirits. Then he said to me, 'Come on, Paul, I'm going to take you somewhere really nice and classy. Just you and me.' I thought that sounded brilliant, so I jumped in the taxi with him and the bastard took us all the way back to the hotel. Fair enough, I thought, time for bed.

The next day, me birthday, the gaffer said I could have the morning to myself, but I had to be back by 1 p.m. I decided to have a quiet drink so off I went, looking stylish in me England tracksuit and Dr. Martens, and found a little bar. I was having a grand time, smoking a huge cigar and drinking champagne, when I notice the time. It was one o'clock already, so I jumped in a cab and arrived back at the hotel an hour late, in the middle of lunch. All the players, management and officials were sitting at a big table when I walked in saying, 'Hi guys. You alright?' I still had me cigar and a bottle of bubbly with me. The gaffer just shook his head as if to say, 'Look at the state of you.' He had a word with us later, mind, telling us to calm down.

We were leaving the next day and on the plane back I got a bit tiddly. We were making a bit of noise, being a bit boisterous I admit, but it still annoyed me when an official from the FA came upstairs to our compartment and told us to keep it down. I decided to give the bloke a piece of my mind so I charged downstairs and confronted him. 'You been upstairs? Telling my England team what to do? Well listen, you're not England. I'm England, we're England. Upstairs. Don't ever come up again without asking permission of the England players. We are England.' It was a stupid rant brought on by too much to drink of course. After I was finished I went back upstairs, told the lads we were sound, and crashed out.

Sound? I don't think so. When we landed back home, fuck me, the shit hit the fan. I was all over the headlines: 'Gazza out of control, Gazza is a disgrace'. There were stories of how we had damaged the plane, all that. I got the worst of it, with people saying I should be chucked out of the team. So I thought I had better lie low for a bit.

We had a few days off before the tournament, so I took myself away to a health farm and then for a quiet spot of fishing in Wales. I'd heard about a hotel that was super-exclusive, where Hugh Grant had hidden, unbothered by the press after his little incident with that nice girl who was standing on the street corner in LA. When I called up for a room the owner assured me no one would ever find us. Fat chance.

I arrived, dumped my bags and was off to the river bank as quickly as I could. Lovely. For about five minutes. I was just beginning to relax when the owner reappeared, out of breath and clearly agitated. 'Paul, you're not going to believe it. I've got about thirty photographers outside the hotel.' That's what it was like back then. Everyone wanted a piece of us. 'Get my suitcase,' I said to him, 'and meet me on the other side of the lake.' I got into a little boat and rowed across. He met us with my gear and I decided I'd be better off back in Newcastle, where I'd get less bother.

The break did me good. By the time we were set to meet up again for the tournament at the England team hotel I felt relaxed and fit. On arrival at Burnham Beaches there was a nice surprise waiting for me. It was a present from Chris Evans, a CD player which he'd signed and a copy of the 'Three Lions' single. The moment I got into my room I put it by the open window and blasted it out. I could see a couple of the lads' windows open and soon the whole block was listening and singing along. It was a great way to kick things off. The sun was shining, our spirits were up and we were ready to take on the best in Europe in front of our home fans. What could be better?

I think I overdid it, trying to impress the gaffer with me star jumps in training.

SWITZERLAND

That CD from Chris got a lot of play over the following two and a bit weeks. Every morning at the hotel it was my wake-up call to the boys and then we had it again on our way to the matches. It gave the whole team a lift. Still gives me a tingle when I hear it now.

I was determined to enjoy every minute of the tournament, to savour and remember every second because I didn't know if it was going to be my last chance with England. When everyone got off the bus at Wembley for our opening match I hung back and played

'Just like the song said, football really did feel like it was coming home.'

the song one more time. Just me and the three lions.

When the players went off to the dressing room, I decided to walk up the tunnel to savour the atmosphere. The sight that greeted me was breath-taking, with the whole stadium singing and flags waving everywhere. It was astonishing. Just like the song said, football really did feel like it was coming home. I am not sure if having a sneaky peek was the right thing to do though. It got me in a strange mood thinking about how much it meant to all those supporters. I found it difficult to shake off afterwards.

During the match, I knew I wasn't having my greatest game. I was working hard and trying me best but it just wasn't quite happening. The whole team were a bit like that. I think the occasion got to us.

It was a tight match with not a lot of space.

I was substituted with twenty minutes to go. I sat next to Robbie Fowler on the bench and I could see he was looking down at his side, at something in his hand. I asked him what he was doing and he showed me this mini TV. 'Brilliant. We can watch the replays.' 'Sorry Gaz. I'm not watching the game. It's the racing. I've got a horse running.' I was pissing meself.

The game ended in a one-all draw. Not a disaster but not the start we'd been looking for. Afterwards the gaffer gave us a little pep talk but he didn't speak to me directly. He knew I'd be disappointed in my own performance and would need some time to myself. That was his style – never pushing us when it wasn't going to do any good.

I wonder what's happening at Newmarket?

SCOTLAND

A couple of nights before the Scotland game I couldn't sleep. I kept going over the first match in my head, worrying that I was going to be dropped. At 11.30 p.m. I knocked on the gaffer's door. He was in his dressing gown. 'What's the matter? Come on in.'

'I know I didn't do well in the first game and I'm worried I am not going to get picked for the next one.'

'Well, it's true, you didn't have the best of games.'

'I know, I know. I can't sleep thinking about it. Am I playing or not?'

'Come on, Paul, you know I don't pick the team until the day before.'

'Please, Gaffer, tell us. It's Scotland. I'll do me best. I'll play much better.'

'I'm just not too sure, Gaz... I think I need a cup of tea.' It was killing us. We chatted about the Switzerland game but there was only one thing I was really interested in. After about forty-five minutes I think the gaffer had had his fun. He smiled and said, 'Of course I'm playing you. I couldn't leave you out. Now off you go. Get some sleep. You've got an important match in two days.'

That gave me a right boost. It was just what I needed and all the next day I was smiling whenever I saw him, 'Cheers, Gaffer. I owe you one.' I'm like that. Whenever someone does us a favour I like to pay them back and I think I can say I did that in the game.

The game got underway and I felt comfortable. I was doing what I had to do, playing well and following the instructions I'd been given at training. The first half wasn't that thrilling, with the Scots probably marginally having the upper hand, but then everything changed when the teams emerged for the second half. We went one up in the fifty-third minute thanks to a back post header from Shearer and the momentum was definitely with us. Then Scotland got a penalty.

I couldn't believe it. I didn't want to look but at the last moment I turned round, dropped my hands and saw Dave Seaman make a great save. Suddenly I had to be alert. Everything was happening very fast. They took a quick corner, there was a foul in the box and Seaman belted the free kick up the park. Teddy picked it up and slipped a pass to Darren Anderton who flicked it through to me as I made a move towards their box.

As the ball was coming over I took a quick glance and saw Colin Hendry charging towards us. I could tell he was out to make a challenge rather than looking to stop and block my run in on goal. If he had been I'd have had no choice but to control the ball on the deck and take him on. But he was moving too fast so I quickly made up my mind what I was going to do. The moment I saw his shadow out the corner of my eye I knocked the ball over his head. He wasn't expecting that and he did his best to put the brakes on. But all he managed was to end up on his arse. Then it was just a matter of hitting the target. I knew I'd have to make good contact to beat their keeper Andy Goram, so I kept my eye on the ball and hit it low. Cracking in volleys like that was something I'd done in training a lot, but to do it at Wembley, in a major tournament, against our oldest rivals, that was something else. Something very special.

Prior to the game, I said to the guys, 'Whoever scores should do the dentist chair.' Shearer had got the first one but he was a bit superstitious about changing his raised-arm celebration so it was down to me. I remembered just in time, when I saw the water bottles lying by the goal. To be honest, it was a bit of a 'fuck you' to the press who had been shouting for me to be dropped. I lay on me back and screamed 'Yes! Yes! Yes!' at the top of me voice as the lads squirted us with the water. Brilliant.

Back in Glasgow I never once mentioned the goal, even though the Rangers lads had been giving me a load of grief beforehand about how they were going to slaughter us. I didn't want to rub it in, I didn't need to. They all knew just how good it was.

'I lay on me back and screamed 'Yes! Yes! Yes!' at the top of me voice as the lads squirted us with the water. Brilliant.'

HOLLAND

Terry Venables was a fantastic coach. His training methods throughout the whole tournament were second to none. That was particularly true in the days leading up to the Holland match. We knew how good they were technically so we worked on different aspects to counter that, especially defence. Naturally I wasn't too amused to begin with.

'Why can't I do some shooting?'

'No, I need you to work on this, Gaz. If you're going to score you're going to score. I can leave that up to you, but if we don't concede we can't get beat!'

My job when we didn't have possession was to get in the way, niggle and be a pain in the arse whenever the ball came into the pocket of the pitch I was in charge of. That's how Terry liked to play me. I was to block any passes and stop the through ball. If nothing came

my way I stayed put so I was free when we got the ball back. The gaffer used to tell the others, 'If you win the ball, look for Gazza straight away.'

Everyone had a different role and Terry made sure these became second nature. Even if subs were brought on, the rest of us knew precisely how the system had to adapt with the new player because Terry had made sure we had worked on every eventuality in training. It became automatic.

In a way, I felt I had a point to prove in this match. I knew they had players with incredible ability but I felt I could match them in every department and I wanted to show the world that an Englishman was just as skilful as any Dutchman – perhaps more so. As it turned out, this proved to be one of my best games for England. I didn't make it easy for myself, mind. I forgot me boots.

I was in the changing room when I realised I'd left them in the hotel. There was no way I could go back to pick them up, so I quietly had a look round to see who I might be able to borrow from. Sheringham's looked about the same size as mine. 'Teddy,' I whispered, 'can I have a word? I've forgotten me boots. You must have a spare pair in your bag.'

'Aye, I've got a pair, but they're a bit ripped.'

'Doesn't matter. Give them here. What size are you?'
'Ten and a half.'

'Shit, I'm a nine but they'll have to do.' I had a look at them and they weren't just a bit ripped, they were totally knackered. I was worried me sock was going to slip out during the match so I got some Sellotape and wound it around me foot before I put the boot on. In the picture at the start of this section, the one where I've totally skinned that Dutch bloke, you can just about make out where me left boot is coming apart. There was no way they were going to last the match so before half-time I got word to the bench that I'd need a new pair which they found from somewhere. You can see in the photo with Tony Adams in the second half that I'm wearing a different pair, with a red tongue this time.

I always tried to stand next to Paul Ince as we lined up because that's pretty much how we played together on the pitch. He would shadow us. If ever I was tackled, he would be there to pick up the ball and give it straight back to us so I could go again. I felt sorry for him sometimes because I only needed to do one or two things well, or score a goal, and I'd get all the headlines, whereas he'd put the graft in and was never fully appreciated for it.

I was buzzing before the kick off against Holland. In the tunnel I'd looked across at the Dutch team and thought, I don't fear you. I've played against Van Basten, Rijkaard, Gullit, Koeman and we had held them. This Holland side were a good team, don't get me wrong, with Bergkamp, Seedorf, De Boer, but I was confident we were better and I felt sharp and fit. The Scotland game had given me a big boost and I just wanted to get on the ball as much as possible.

I started the game well and was enjoying my tussles with Seedorf. At one point I put me foot on the ball and invited him to come and get it off us. I always enjoyed talking to defenders who were man-marking us, to wind them up and distract them. I'd come out with things like, 'I've been seeing your girlfriend.' If they claimed they didn't have a girlfriend I'd say, 'Yes you do, she's in the stand.' Then I'd point and if they glanced, even for a fraction of a second, I'd be past them and away. Sometimes I'd drive them so mental they would swap markers, to get a break.

Shearer had scored a penalty to put us one up at half-time. I then had a hand in the next two. Teddy got his head to me corner for our second and then for the third, I picked up the ball from McManaman, held off my old Lazio team-mate Aron Winter and slipped the ball to Teddy, who moved it on to Shearer to slam home. Nice.

One thing stood out in that game. In general, even when the fans are all there for England, supporting the national team brilliantly, club rivalries can sometimes surface. So for instance, a Man United player might play a loose pass and you can hear Liverpool fans giving him some stick. Or if an Arsenal player makes a mistake, the Spurs supporters will have a go at him. It is perfectly normal and all part of the banter of football.

I'd certainly been on the receiving end of that in the past, but in that Holland game it was different. Ninety thousand fans were singing, 'One Paul Gascoigne.' It was ringing in me ears. I remember David Platt came on as sub and I passed him the ball but he came running over and gave it back to me. 'Come on,' he said, 'you take it. It's your game.' I gave myself a moment then, just to stand still in the middle of the pitch and soak it all in before getting on with the match.

When Teddy put us four-nil up I was saying to our guys, 'Come on. Keep at it. We can help get Scotland through.' I knew Coisty had scored for them in the first half and if they went on to win against Switzerland it was going to come down to goal difference. The Scots lads were mates and I wanted them to make it through, so I was disappointed when Kluivert scored his goal to make it 4–1. In the end, that put Scotland out. I didn't dwell on it, mind. We'd taken the Dutch apart and were on our way to the quarter-finals. I didn't think anyone could beat us.

On the final whistle Tony Adams came over to us. 'That's got to be one of the best performances I've ever seen, Gazza. Make sure you keep yourself right for the next one. We need you.' I really appreciated that. Tony was a great captain and knew how to motivate his players. He was always encouraging and supportive. During a game you always knew where Tony was because he would be screaming his head off the whole time – you couldn't escape it. He used to get so worked up and high-pitched he sounded like a lass.

CHAPTER 11

NEVER STOP DREAMING

EURO '96: KNOCKOUT STAGE

SPAIN

T he one worry after smashing the Dutch like we did might have been complacency but Terry Venables made sure that wasn't going to happen. He knew how good the Spanish were from his days at Barcelona, and he kept drumming it into us. They were playing well, looked fit and each one of them was comfortable on the ball.

In big matches it is important to show no fear.

To counter this Terry adopted slightly different tactics. Instead of looking to close them down quickly which we had been doing up to then in the matches, he told us to play more on the counter-attack. 'If you get too tight,' he said, 'they will play the ball round you and we'll be on the back foot.' He liked to play in a consistent style normally, but occasionally he would twist things slightly when he thought it necessary to surprise the opposition.

In the end it wasn't exactly a classic. I think we cancelled each other out, both sides wary of the other team. Dave Seaman was brilliant throughout the game, making some important stops and controlling everything. Our tactics meant we were defending deep, outside our own box. You could hear Dave the whole time, shouting instructions, making sure we were properly organised. Knowing your keeper is on top of things gives you a huge amount of confidence. To me, this is the match where Dave made his name as one of the best keepers in the world.

Due to the style of play it was inevitable that it went to penalties. We'd been practising them hard because Terry knew that if the match went to extra time, there was a fair chance that with ten minutes to go the Spanish would sit back and settle for the spot-kick lottery.

I was confident that I would score. After all, even though this was me first major penalty shoot-out, wasn't I the Gateshead Schools champion? How could I fail with that sort of pedigree?

Walking up to take your kick is a strange experience. There are two ways it can go. If you are taking the penalty towards your own fans then behind the goal is silent. All you can see is the expressions of hope on the faces. If you are up at the other end all you get is shouting and jeering. That's how it was against Spain but at least at the old Wembley there was a fair distance between the pitch and the crowd so all you could really see was the bank of photographers. You just hope no one takes a flash as you are about to hit the ball...

So I was walking up thinking, stay calm, stay calm, but it was difficult. There were a hundred things going through me mind: the twenty thousand people directly in front of me, staring at my face; the players and staff staring at my back; the cameras; what it would feel like to score, or miss; how I was going to celebrate... As I put the ball down I focused on one thing: score for the lads, we are in this together.

Then, just before I took the kick I imagined it was just me there, in an empty park. All that was in front of me was a rusty set of posts, no net. I didn't think about the players, the fans, the cameras. It was about hitting the spot I'd decided on, low and hard. Give the keeper no chance. Then I am running up.

I gave it a quick glance to me right to put the keeper off, hoping he was looking at my eyes, then I hit it left. I think I did him straight away with the eyes and me body movement because he hardly moved – he just sort of fell over! When the ball went in, the release of tension was explosive. My penalty made it 4–2 to us. If they missed the next it was all over.

I am not sure Dave Seaman actually realised that. When he saved it he jumped up as if to say, 'Yeah, I got that one', not realising we were through. It was only when he saw us charging towards him that the penny dropped. He was the star, no doubt about it. Two penalty saves in the tournament – you can't ask for more than that.

We were in the semis and even better (sort of), the gaffer had given us a couple of days off. Dave Seaman and I had it all planned. We were going fishing.

HOOKED

It was a beautiful day, warm and sunny, and I was looking forward to a peaceful few hours on the lake accompanied by a half dozen bottles of hooch. Perfect. Well, almost. I'd been having trouble sleeping throughout the tournament so a few of the lads had given me some tablets to try. I'd built up a small stash so I decided to whack down a couple, just to make sure I was nice and relaxed. They worked a treat.

Dave Seaman tells me he'd never seen anything like it before. We'd been there about half an hour, I was in me waders, fishing away in the sunshine when all of a sudden – boom! The next thing I knew I was on the bank, soaking wet. The combination of the pills and the hooch had done for me. Apparently I wobbled for a second and then I fell face first into the water, totally out of it. Dave had to rush over and drag us out. As far as I was concerned he was a hero. He saved me life. After he'd stopped pissing himself, he says.

There was no way I could continue so we went back to the hotel and I crashed out for a couple of hours. I woke up in the afternoon and fancied a game of snooker but I couldn't find anyone. I was searching in the grounds when I noticed smoke drifting up from behind some hedges. I thought it was a fire and I ran round to see what I could do.

So I went behind the hedge to find out what was going on, only to discover it wasn't a fire at all, just a bunch of the players having a crafty fag and a few bottles of Bud. They were obviously having a good laugh so I decided to join them. Up to then I'd never really smoked. I might have had the odd puff when I was a bairn but not properly. I took a good drag. That's a nice feeling, I thought. I like that. That was me hooked. I'd have saved meself a fortune over the years if I'd stayed out fishing that day instead of having a kip in the lake. Oh well.

Fire! fire!

We went fishing again the next day and I promised we'd do it properly. Dave was on one peg and I was on the next. We weren't alone but that was fine, no one was paying us any attention. Then I notice there was a bloke clearly only pretending to fish. He didn't have a clue what he was doing. 'You're press, you,' I shouted. He looked startled, grabbed his gear and ran to his car, leaving behind his mobile phone. I chased after him and as he was fumbling to open the boot to dump his stuff I ran past and locked the wooden gates at the entrance to the lake. He looked shit scared, panicking and unable to start the car so I tried to let down his tyres. As I was crouching there he got the engine fired up and whoosh, shot straight through the gates, smashing them to pieces and almost taking me finger with him.

By then Dave had caught up with us. 'You daft little berk', he used strong language did Dave, 'that could have been you out of the semi-final.' He was right. It was a stupid thing to do, but I hated the fact that the press were being so underhand after all the crap that had been dished out to me following Hong Kong. A little later the gaffer called. 'Everything alright there, lads? No bother?' 'No, no, just a photographer but he's gone now.' Then the bloke's phone went. It was the police.

They asked us to stay where we were and they would come and pick it up. They did, and we managed to keep the whole thing quiet. We even went back there a couple of times in the evenings after training, taking a boat with Ian Walker once (who is in the photo), but we were careful not to do anything else daft. When I say 'we', of course I actually mean me.

GERMANY

After the fishing exploits it was back to business. We were facing Germany and both Stuart Pearce and me felt we owed them one for 1990. You could see how much it meant to Psycho. In the four days between the Spain game and the semi he had his angry face on pretty much the whole time.

In training we again concentrated on defensive work, but this time we were looking to close them down quickly because we knew that is what they would do with us. We also worked on set pieces and as an example of how thorough the gaffer was, he hired one of those cherry picker things, put a cameraman up there and filmed the training session so we could see everyone's movement properly. Then he would get some of our players to play like the Germans, fourteen of them against eleven of us, so we had to be incredibly sharp to keep tight on them.

The gaffer was brilliant at encouraging us and building our confidence. There was never any of the 'Remember the war' crap. It was all about how we were better than them, how we could beat them playing the way we had been, that it wasn't a fluke we were in the semi-finals – we deserved it.

When we arrived at the stadium the fans sitting inside seemed to sense we were there and a roar like nothing I'd heard before burst out of the ground. Perhaps they could hear the chain on the massive wooden gates being pulled back to let the coach in. There was something about those gates. When they opened up and you drove through, that's when your heart started going at a hundred miles an hour. When they closed behind you, I always looked back to watch. It was like being admitted to the Colosseum. You felt that there was no way out if you didn't get the right result.

'You could see how much it meant to Psycho.
In the four days between the Spain game
and the semi he had his angry face on
pretty much the whole time.'

We got off to a great start. Three minutes in, we got awarded a corner. Adams' flick, and Shearer's header meant we were one up. I thought we had them then. Everyone was playing brilliantly. I was doing what I had to do. I wasn't man-marking because the gaffer wanted me to stay free but I still had massive defensive duties, helping Incey out a lot more in this game to give him some space, plus supporting the front two.

They levelled with a good goal after quarter of an hour and from then on both sides had chances to win it. In extra time it was the golden goal and Darren Anderton was incredibly unlucky not to finish the match off when he hit the post, then they had a goal disallowed. Time was ticking towards penalties when Teddy knocked the ball wide to Shearer on the right. I still think about what happened next to this day. I hate it. I just keep thinking, if only.

Shearer whipped the ball across the box. As I went for it, I hesitated for a split second, and that was it. I couldn't reach it. It was inches. Less even. The truth is, Shearer or Lineker would have put it away. They were natural goal scorers, their vision on the pitch was different from mine. I thought the keeper was going to get a touch and I tried to anticipate that. Shearer and Lineker wouldn't have thought about the keeper. They would have just concentrated on the ball. If it had been the other way round, my pass and Shearer in the box, we'd have been in the final.

It is strange the things that can flash across your mind even as a move is unfolding. Just as Shearer had hit his pass, before I thought about the keeper, I was sure I was going to score and I had me celebration all worked out. I was going to run past the goal, all the way round the track, down the tunnel, dive into the bath and come back soaking wet. But as it was I just lay there, thinking, 'Fuck me, an inch, an inch. I can't believe it.'

NEVER STOP DREAMING

So to penalties again, against the Germans. The one thing I had been desperate to avoid. The score was 3–3 when I walked up to take mine. I had a tear in me eye as I approached the ball. I was terrified I'd miss. I dared not look across at Dave Seaman. We were good mates and he always made us laugh. This wasn't the moment for a fit of the giggles. I thought, come on Paul, pull yourself together. Just do what you normally do. Don't try to be clever. Same as you did against Spain. A glance to the right to throw the keeper, and knock it low and hard to the left.

But just as I was about to take it the keeper moved and I changed me mind. I got it all wrong and struck the ball with me ankle and it flew into the top right-hand corner. It looked like one of the best spot kicks taken that day, but in truth I fluked it.

The relief when I scored was incredible.

Come on Dave. Save it. Get us through.

At 5–5 each, Gareth Southgate missed. That's it, I thought, twice now I've lost out to the Germans on penalties. They still had to take theirs but with the pressure off to some extent, Andreas Moller wasn't about to blow it. They scored and it was all over. I slumped down, my 'what if' moment from earlier spinning around in me head.

As we walked towards our supporters I said to Gareth, 'Don't worry about it. There will be a next time.' But perhaps not for me, I thought. I felt for Gareth because he wasn't really a penalty taker but he had the guts to take it. No one blamed him at all. He was obviously distraught so later I tried to cheer him up. 'Come on, Gareth, think on the bright side. The England rugby boys got slaughtered by that massive Lomu bloke and they did alright. I bet you get a pizza advert out of this just like them.' I can't remember if he laughed or not.

Not again.

In the changing room Terry spoke to us with passion, saying that we had done our country proud. They hadn't beaten us in the game itself and that we had done everything wo oould. Now it was lime, he said, to go back to the hotel and try and enjoy ourselves for the last night. The fans were waiting for us when we arrived back and the reception they gave us was fantastic. We were obviously bitterly disappointed but seeing them cheer and clap gave us a boost. They knew we had given our all.

NEVER STOP DREAMING

CHAPTER 12

GOING OFF
THE RAILS

RANGERS:
JULY 1996 – MARCH 1998

got married to Sheryl on 1 July 1996. It was a good summer. I'd had a great first season with Rangers and in Euro '96, England had got to within a penalty kick of reaching the final. The wedding itself was a brilliant day, our friends and family were there and we were happy. I was looking forward to the start of the season. Everything seemed to be on the up.

In the first Old Firm encounter of the new campaign I scored one of my all-time favourite goals. Before the game, Shel had asked whether we were going to go out that evening and I told her that it would depend on the result. When you are playing in such high-profile matches and you lose, it can be hard to lift yourself after to socialise. So I didn't want to promise and then be a pain in the arse all evening if we'd lost.

Richard Gough opened the scoring with a fantastic header and Celtic really started going for it after that. In one attack they hit the bar and I picked up the rebound on the edge of the box. I thought about knocking it wide straight away to Jorg Albertz on the wing, but I saw a gap and I knew I could get past the two Celtic attackers. I kept going and reached the halfway line. Then I ran out of steam.

'I was looking forward to the start of the season. Everything seemed to be on the up.'

The Old Firm matches were always draining, all big derbies are. It's as if you are playing two matches in ninety minutes. The first is all about the adrenalin flowing through you which can knacker you even before you step on the pitch. Then you've got the game itself. In massive matches like this you are so shit-scared of letting in a goal or making a mistake that your nerves can get the better of you. It might sound daft, but sometimes it is a relief if you go one down, because that worry about fucking up is suddenly lifted and all your energies are focused on getting a goal back. As we were one up, that release of pressure wasn't there and I was beginning to feel the strain.

Thinking I'd done my bit, I sent the ball out to Albertz assuming he would waste some time and allow the others to catch up. But he didn't and I realised it was only me forward so I had to keep going. I arrived in the box just as Albertz hit a fabulous cross. As the ball was coming over I thought the defender was going to beat me to it, but it was too quick for him. I've never been the best header of a ball so I just threw meself at it and luckily made great contact. It went past the keeper like a bullet. I knew where Shel was in the stadium so I picked meself up and ran over there to give her a message. 'We're going out, we're going out!'

We're going out!

A month after that goal everything went horribly wrong. This book is about my football career, so I deliberately haven't gone into some of the harder times in my life off the pitch, the drinking and other things. But there is one incident that I do need to touch on. I was responsible for physically hurting my wife in an incident at the Gleneagles hotel. It was the worst thing I've ever done and I make no excuses for my actions. They are indefensible. This book, however, isn't the place to go into what happened. I've done that elsewhere. But what I do think is relevant here is how my appalling behaviour that Saturday night subsequently affected me on the pitch.

Rangers were playing Ajax away in the Champions League on the following Tuesday. Throughout my time in Glasgow we had very little success in that tournament and this match was no exception. People always say it was because the quality of football in Scotland wasn't good enough, but I think that's bollocks. We tended to do alright at home, certainly holding our own, but away we were invariably slaughtered. For whatever reason, we failed to raise our game when it mattered, partly I think because in Scotland there weren't that many foreign players at the time and we were unused to different styles of play. It was okay at home, when we could dictate, but on the road we failed to adapt. It had nothing to do with the level of play in Scotland.

We were flying out on Monday and all day Sunday I was worrying about what I had done to Shel, how I had hurt her. No one knew anything about it at this stage, so I was bottling it up inside. In many ways, when it did hit the papers a day or so later, it was a relief. At least then I could face up to my actions and try to make amends.

I should have told Walter what happened, I know that now. But at the time I was too scared. So I really wasn't thinking straight by the time kick off came around, not helped by the fact that the gaffer decided to play me up front, which wasn't my usual position. It was one more thing messing with me head.

Ajax went one up after twenty-five minutes and not long after the red mist descended. I kicked Winston Bogarde, pretty much up the arse, and I was sent off. I was so ashamed of myself for the stupidity of the 'tackle' and for everything that was going on, that when the lads came in at half-time I tried to hide in the toilets. Richard Gough was having none of it. He kicked in the door and had a right go at me. 'What the fuck are you doing! We needed you out there and you get sent off for such a fucking stupid thing.' I broke down at that

moment and told him I'd beaten up my wife. I think by then I knew the press had got hold of the story and it was only a matter of time before it all came out.

Goughy was brilliant. He didn't in any way condone what I had done but he said he would help in any way he could. That was the sort of spirit we had in the team. I'd let them down in all sorts of ways but the captain didn't abandon me. I have been lucky to play with some great leaders in my career, Butcher, Mabbutt, Robson, and Richard Gough is right up there. He would put his head in where others wouldn't put their feet. He was an inspiration.

I also explained everything to Walter. 'Why didn't you tell me before? We could have organised things but now you are going to have to face the press at the airport. You need to apologise and then we can begin to move on.'

Quite rightly, I got crucified in the press and all I could do was just as Walter had said. Apologise and try to start rebuilding things.

Our next match was against Aberdeen. The pressure was really on in that game and as I walked out on to the pitch I did my best to block out everything else apart from football. Not surprisingly, the opposition fans were giving us a load of grief, chanting that I was a wife beater, holding up red cards, everything they could to put us off. On the pitch, if you stand still then it gets to you, but if you keep busy, go looking for the ball, you don't hear the crowd.

In the Aberdeen game we got a free kick about twenty-five yards out and I said to the guys that I fancied it. They could see in me eyes what it meant to me. I bent it over the wall into the opposite corner. That put the red cards down for about a minute, but that wasn't as important as the feeling that I had taken at least one small step towards making amends to some of the people I had let down.

So that's how I set about trying to get through this difficult period. In each match I did me best to be involved as much as possible. It seemed to work. In the next game I got a hat trick against Motherwell in our 5–0 win. Slowly, the darkness that was surrounding me began to lift. One match in particular around this time sticks in my mind – when Andy Goram saved me arse.

I owe you big time, Andy

The game was in the league against Celtic, at their place. They were sitting at the top of the table so it was crucial we got something out of the game. Laudrup had put us one up with a belter inside the first ten minutes and that's how it stayed for the next hour. Then, running on to a through-ball from me, Brian was brought down by the Celtic keeper and it was left to me to finish off the game from the spot. It has got to have been the worst penalty I have ever taken. Me gran could have saved it – with her eyes closed. I felt bad enough after I'd missed it, but I felt a whole lot worse when, with only five minutes to go, they got a penalty themselves. If they scored, they'd remain on top. Having worked so hard to let me football do the talking over the previous few weeks, I felt I'd screwed everything up with that one miss.

Van Hooijdonk took it. He struck it well, low and hard to his left, but Goram was more than up to it. He made a fantastic save – winning the game for us, putting us top of the league, and getting me off the hook. Andy was always a brilliant keeper – one of the best I've ever played alongside – but this was even more impressive than normal because he'd been out for a month. Not that you would have known from the way he played. He was immense.

BREAKING HEARTS

I was desperate to give something back to the Rangers fans after all the support they'd given us, and the 1996 League Cup final against Hearts seemed the perfect opportunity. Only trouble was, I was too desperate. I got meself all worked up beforehand (where have I heard that before) and played, and acted, like a bit of an arse in the first half. I made a couple of half-decent runs but I didn't feel I was getting involved enough.

Ally had put us two up inside the first half an hour, which was brilliant of course, but it was no thanks to me. Coisty and I just weren't clicking. If I went to play him through, he didn't make the run. If I wanted to play it short for a one-two, he was moving into the space. At one stage, on the edge of the box, I saw a gap and slipped it through to Ally, which would have been great if he'd been there! He was holding his ground, waiting to play off me. It was frustrating and I let it show, throwing me arms up in despair, shaking me head and giving it the universal 'you're mental' gesture.

Coisty was not impressed. He chased me up the park, grabbed the back of me neck and said if I ever did that again he'd have me. I was so wound up that I gave him some back, squaring up to him. Ridiculous really, but it spilled over into the tunnel and dressing room at half-time, both of us acting like kids in a playground. I soon realised that I was in the wrong and calmed down, apologising to Coisty.

In the dressing room, Archie took me to one side. 'Have you had a drink?'

'No Archie, honestly, I haven't.'

'Well go and get one.' That surprised me, but I wasn't going to say no. Off I went to the players' lounge, where all the directors were, and called over the barman. 'Give us a triple brandy, mate. Quick as possible.' I knocked it back in a oner, felt great and went out and scored two goals in two minutes after they had pulled it back to 2–2. I felt a bit bad about those goals mind you. It can't have been too much fun for the lads getting a whiff of me breath when they were congratulating us.

3–2

'I was desperate to give something back to the Rangers fans after all the support they'd given us.'

4–2, but don't get too close.

Coisty and me make up.
Two goals each in our
4–3 win.

SUPER ALLY

Coisty was brilliant to play with and what a laugh we had! We got on from the very beginning. He was one of the first of the lads to take me for a pint, and there was a nice bit of good-natured rivalry because he'd played for Sunderland and I was Newcastle. A Mackem versus a Geordie always adds something extra. Some people think of Coisty as a classic poacher, a bit like Gary Lineker, but the truth is he could finish from anywhere. Brilliant headers, shots from outside the box – Ally had it all.

He also had a fantastic football brain. Sometimes the way I played caused me problems because I was thinking further ahead than me team-mates, but I met my match with Coisty. He was like me, working three moves out in advance, which meant we developed a fantastic partnership.

And fuck me, did we have some fun. One Bonfire Night, I spent £300 on the biggest rockets I could find. You could have hitched a ride to the moon on these things. I called up Ally at home – he only lived a couple of miles away. 'Coisty, I've got a present for you,' I said.

'Cheers Gaz, what is it?'

'I'll send it through now.'

I put one of the rockets on my fence and aimed it towards his house and set it off. Whoosh! Jimmy was with me and we were crying with laughter. A minute later Coisty's on the phone. 'What the hell is going on at my house?' I told him and we were both laughing…until the police turned up. 'The woman at the bottom of the drive called,' they said. 'She was worried that someone was trying to shoot you. Is everything okay?' I tried to talk me way out of it but I had no chance. The rocket I was trying to hide behind me back and the two in the fence ready for launch were a dead giveaway. They said they'd have to arrest me if I didn't stop. I didn't think Walter would have seen the funny side of that.

> '*I met my match with Coisty. He was like me, working three moves out in advance, which meant we developed a fantastic partnership.*'

In one match against Celtic, Coisty scored from one of me crosses so I said to him after the match that we should go out and celebrate. We agreed to meet at lunchtime in a pub the next day. Jimmy and I arrived at 12.30 a.m. There was no sign of Ally by 1.30 p.m., and an hour later than that he still hadn't arrived. The bastard's not coming, I said to Jim, but I'll get him back. It was an hour or so before his kids got home from school so we raced to a local pet shop and bought a rabbit in a cage, two budgies and some tropical fish. I tried to get a sheep but they didn't have any in stock. Then it was quickly round to Coisty's place to leave the presents on the doorstep. I knew once the kids saw them there was no way they could send them back. I was right. Poor Coisty ended up having to feed the rabbit every morning before training. The kids appreciated our gesture, though. They named the budgies Gazza and Jimmy.

NINE-IN-A-ROW

The League Cup final was probably the highlight of me second season at Rangers. Two months later, in January 1997, we were playing in a six-a-side tournament in Amsterdam and I took a knock on me ankle. I didn't think it was too serious but quickly it began to swell up and I was flown home.

Although the swelling did go down a bit, me ankle had to be put in plaster to protect it. I was lying on my back in the hospital as the doctor examined me. It was me right ankle that was the problem and after he had a good look at it he left the room for a moment. I was pretty uncomfortable so I turned over on to me stomach, and when he returned the doctor started putting the plaster on me wrong foot! I thought that was hilarious so I let him carry on. But I wasn't laughing very much when he told me later – once he'd done the proper ankle – that the injury was worse than first thought. I was out of action until April.

I made me first appearance back as a sub when we smashed Raith Rovers 6–0, and was on the bench again for the next match, Motherwell at home, where a draw would have clinched Rangers' ninth league title in a row. Walter brought me on in the second half, when we were one down, and after about fifteen minutes I had a chance to level it up but I blew it. The ball broke to us inside the six-yard box but I scuffed me shot and the chance was gone.

I couldn't face the boys after the match. I ended up hiding in the gym, crying me eyes out. I'd fought hard to make it back before the end of the season and I felt it had all been in vain. I was over-reacting a bit, I know, as we still had two games to go but the whole situation just got on top of me.

We ended up securing the record-equalling nine-in-a-row in the next match, against Dundee United at Tannadice. What a feeling that was! Everything suddenly seemed possible. We were champions with a game in hand. We were invincible! Surely there was nothing to stop us going on to achieve an incredible ten-in-a-row the following season.

Ten-in-a-row? Nothing seemed beyond us.

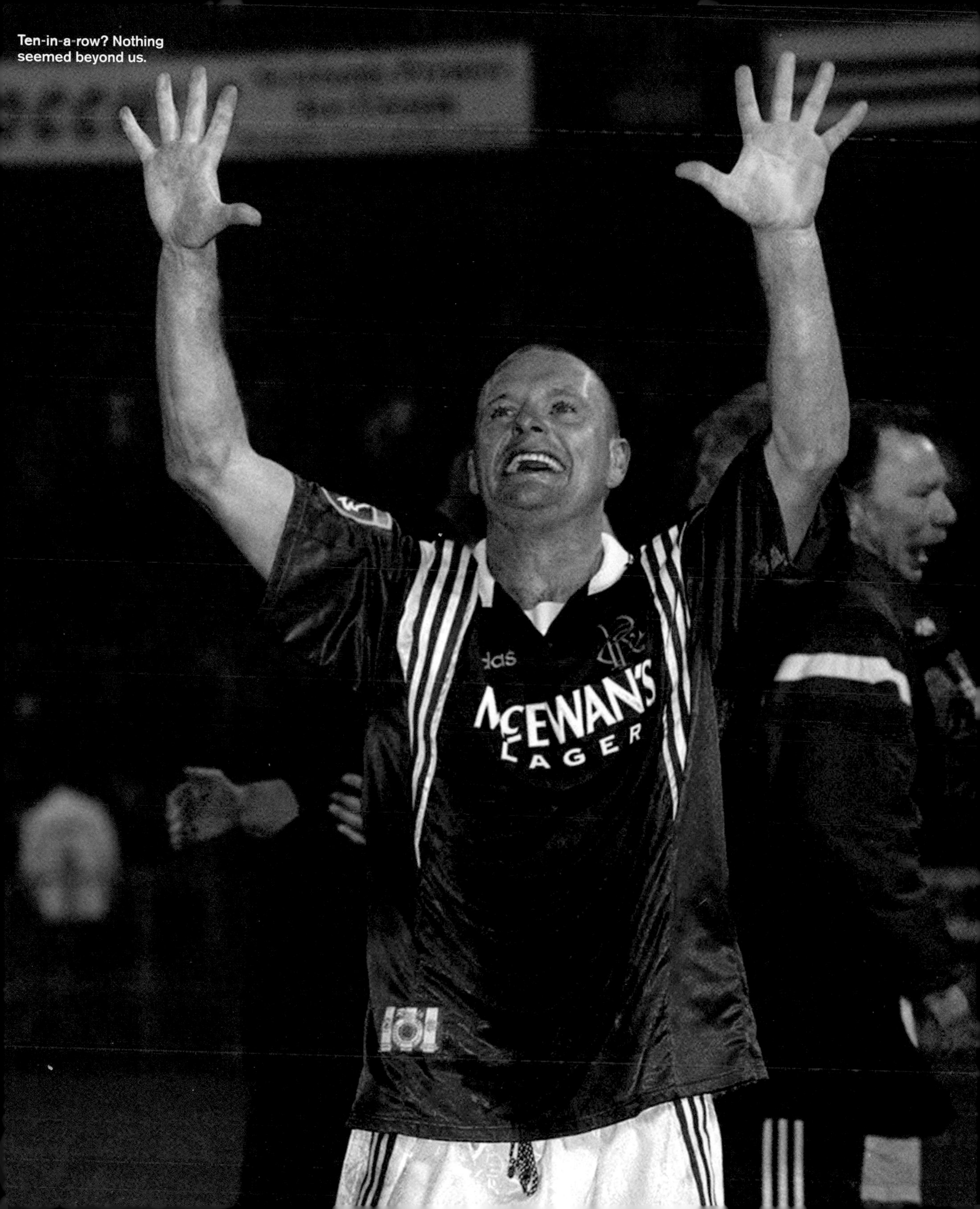

In reality, the Dundee United match marked the beginning of the end for me at Rangers and of the club's most successful era. Not that I, or any of us, knew it at the time. But perhaps I should have seen the signs. That night I went out and got hammered. I was totally out of it, something that was happening too often around then and Walter was getting worried.

Next day at training, he collared me. 'Gazza, I am sick of you and your behaviour! I don't want to see your face again. Get out of this club.' I was shattered and so upset. I thought that was it, there and then. Everything had felt so good less than twenty-four hours previously and now I had gone and blown it. I went home and cried all that day and the next. By the Saturday morning, two days later, Walter still hadn't called, then a couple of hours before the kick off of the final game of the season, away to Hearts, me phone rang. It was Walter.

'Get yourself to Edinburgh. Now.' I jumped into a taxi and when I got to the hotel Walter took me into one of the rooms where there were dozens of empty bottles of champagne littered around. 'What's all this about?' I asked.

'We had a party last night. The whole team except you. You see, Gazza, I tell you when to drink and when not to drink.' I had missed out on the big celebration but at least I understood what Walter was telling me – that my behaviour was well short of what Rangers demanded. Respect was a critical element at the club and I had been in the wrong. That was unacceptable.

'Everything had felt so good less than twenty-four hours previously and now I had gone and blown it. I went home and cried all that day and the next.'

HEADING SOUTH

My high hopes at the end of the previous season had seemed well placed as the 1997/98 campaign got underway. I had signed a new contract, the squad had been strengthened and I felt good in meself. But it didn't last.

Another Champions League exit and a quarter-final defeat by Dundee United in the League Cup were the first indications that all was not well as we went into the Old Firm match in January, although we were still top of the league at that stage.

I'd had a few niggling injuries throughout the first half of the season, missing a number of

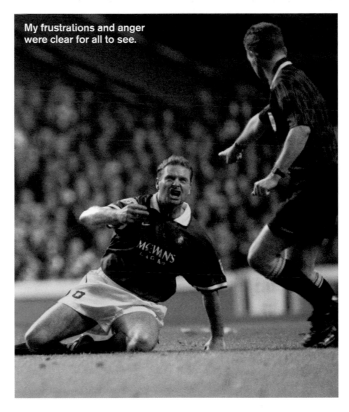

My frustrations and anger were clear for all to see.

games and managing only three goals. I was frustrated and let it show in one of the most stupid things I have ever done. I was on the bench for the match against Celtic and I wasn't happy about it. I was desperate to play and the emotion was boiling over inside me. Walter told us to go and warm up behind the goal where there was a section of Celtic fans, who absolutely slaughtered us. They were calling us every name under the sun.

What I wanted most of all was to get back at them on the pitch, score a goal to silence them. But as that wasn't possible just at that moment (although I did get on later), I reacted in another way. I mimicked the flute again. It was deliberate, provocative and childish. I know I shouldn't have done it. What made things even worse was that it was picked up by Sky TV who were broadcasting the game. The whole world got to see it.

The repercussions were massive. Out driving the following day I pulled up at some traffic lights. The bloke in the car next to me smiled, so I smiled back. He gestured for me to wind down me window and I thought he was going to say something nice, so I did. He pulled out a knife. 'Do that again and I'll fucking slit your throat.'

A few days later, I received a death threat through the post. 'I am going to kill you. My time. My place. You won't be expecting it.' I was crapping meself so I went to the police who took it very seriously. They managed to find out the name and address of the person who had sent the note but as he lived in Dublin, there wasn't anything they could do. But they did give me all these instructions about how to check under me car for bombs, and how to be careful with me mail. I took that to heart. I rang Jimmy and offered him £100 a week if he would do us a favour and open me letters for a while. 'No problem, Paul. I'll come and do that.' I reckoned if anything bad did happen, Jim had enough padding to be okay. Seriously though, we were all incredibly careful with every package that arrived for ages afterwards.

It eventually died down six months later, after I'd left Rangers. The bloke got in contact again to say that as I was no longer at the club and hadn't done it again, the threat was off. That was a relief.

The final nail in me coffin at Rangers was when Walter announced he'd be leaving at the end of the season. The Dutchman Dick Advocaat was going to be taking over and I was worried how I would fit into his plans. So when Walter and then David Murray said they'd received a good offer for me from Bryan Robson at Middlesbrough, I realised it was time to go, although I didn't want to admit it.

I played me last game for Rangers on 21 March 1998, at home against St Johnstone. I didn't know it at the time though. The move down south happened very quickly days afterwards.

I remember looking around the dressing room at Ibrox for the last time, thinking back to the celebrations, the fun, the laughter and most of all, the team spirit. It won't surprise you to learn I was crying. I loved those lads, they'd been so good to me and suddenly this was it. We wouldn't all be together again. But what a time we'd had.

CHAPTER 13

END OF THE
HOLIDAYS

ENGLAND:
SEPTEMBER 1996 – MAY 1998

Terry Venables left the England job after Euro '96 and Glenn Hoddle took over. I must confess, I was a bit worried when I heard who the new gaffer was going to be. Unlike with Terry, I had no previous relationship with Hoddle and I didn't know how he would react to me. My concern was increased when Walter Smith gave me a piece of advice. 'Be careful, Paul,' he said. 'Coming in as the new manager, Hoddle will want to make a name for himself.' He was right.

It all started off okay, though. Hoddle picked us for the first World Cup qualifier, against Moldova in September 1996, and things were looking bright. The team spirit was good, we were still on a high after Euro '96, and there was a sense that the best was yet to come.

The day before the match we went to see the Under-21s play. Just as we got off the coach Paul Ince pulled me shorts down for a laugh so I was determined to get one back on him. It was all good-natured fun. We were sitting in the stands watching the match

when I turned to Incey and said, 'I can't see much from here. Let's climb up into the box – it'll be much better. You go first and I'll give you a bunk up.' Up he went and just as he was about to clamber over I whacked down his tracksuit bottoms. Everyone was pissing themselves and so, to be fair, was Incey. It showed we were still a tight group of lads, even under a new manager.

'Everyone was pissing themselves and so, to be fair, was Incey.'

We did well in the Moldova match, winning 3–0 and I scored a nice looping header which was rare for me. It was me ninth England goal. I thought then I had loads more in me. As it turned out, that was my second last.

Alan Shearer was captain for the first time and he did well. I congratulated him at the end with a big kiss. I am not sure he was too happy about the thought of wearing the armband regularly if that was what he had to put up with.

I got on well with Shearer. We had this funny little routine we used to do. He used to say, 'Come on lads,' and I would always follow it up with, 'Come on England.' I know it sounds daft and a bit childish, but when you are in a team these little things make people laugh and help relieve the tension. I enjoyed playing with Alan. You always knew you were going to get something off him. If he wasn't scoring goals, he'd be making them, giving it 100 per cent for the team.

The other significant thing about the match was that it was David Beckham's debut. When he first joined the England camp he was shy and used to sit at the front of the bus but he couldn't escape me. Once he started seeing Victoria a little bit later, I'd be up the back and I'd start singing, 'Becks, weeell...tell me what you want, what you really, really want.' He was a good lad and used to laugh along with the other guys. 'I've heard about him,' he'd say, 'but now I've actually met the Gaz.'

I used to take the free kicks for England but I knew when Becks joined that he had a reputation as being a bit special with the dead ball. I wanted him to settle in quickly so in matches I used to say to him that he should have a go sometimes. But I only did this in the games themselves. I'm not that daft. If he started thumping them in from every angle at training that would have been the end of me.

I played in the next two qualifiers, against Poland at home and Georgia away. In the Poland game I took a knock and had to be stretchered off. In the dugout, I wanted to phone Sheryl, to see how our new baby was doing, so as the match was going on I sort of hid behind Martin Keown and Tim Flowers to make the call, out of sight of Hoddle. I'd just got through when Tim suddenly decided to do some stretches, dropping me right in it. The gaffer looked across, saw me on the blower and gave a right earful.

In September 1997, I scored me last goal for England. It was in the return qualifier against Moldova at Wembley. I picked up the ball on the halfway line, sucked in about five of their defenders then played a neat exchange with Ian Wright and knocked it past the keeper. If that had to be my final ever international goal, it wasn't a bad one to go out on.

Paul Scholes was playing in that game. You can just see him in the background in this photo. He made his debut earlier in the year and was fast becoming a permanent fixture in the England set-up. What a player he was, one of my favourites of all time. How he plays on the pitch is exactly the way he is in training – down to earth and always giving everything he has. I loved playing with Scholesy, you could give him the ball in any position and he would know exactly what to do with it. Top class.

A few years after this, I was playing in a celebrity golf tournament in Portugal with Dave Seaman. We were down on the beach, relaxing and watching the world go by, when I noticed some kids having a kick about. They looked like they were having a right laugh, but one of them stood out a mile. Fuck me, I thought, he's a bit special. I should get his name and mention him to some clubs when I get home. So I went over and tapped him on the shoulder. 'Excuse me, son,' I said. 'Can I have a word?' He turned round and it was Scholesy. He was laughing his head off.

THE ITALIAN JOB

England's qualifying campaign for the 1998 World Cup in France boiled down to the final group match, away to Italy. To be sure of making it we had to get something out of the game or we would be facing the massive pressure of a play-off.

It felt strange being back in the Olympic Stadium where I'd played for Lazio, but I was determined not to let it get to me. I was fit and confident and had a job to do. We were out to contain the Italians and I was to hold the midfield. Nothing flash, just get the point we needed.

A few months earlier in a friendly against South Africa, I'd had a bit of a row with Hoddle so I knew it was important that I did exactly what I was told. I didn't want to screw up my chances of making it to France if we got past the Italians.

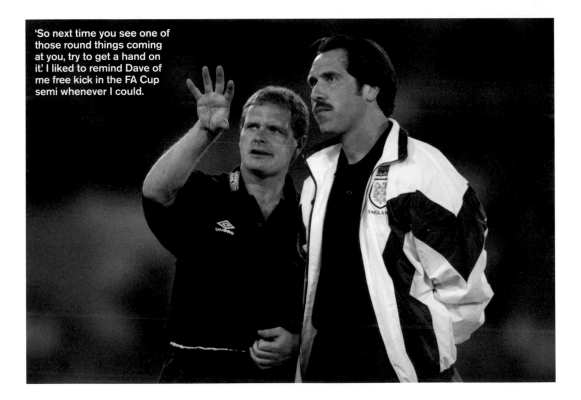

'So next time you see one of those round things coming at you, try to get a hand on it'. I liked to remind Dave of me free kick in the FA Cup semi whenever I could.

In the South Africa match I'd had a bit of a set-to with one of the linesmen, complaining over an offside decision or something. As I'd been 'discussing' it with him I'd noticed he was chewing some nicotine gum and I fancied having a go. Smoking on the pitch is frowned upon but this might be the next best thing, I thought.

At half-time, Hoddle wanted a word with us and asked me to step into a certain room. I couldn't be arsed getting a lecture so I deliberately went through the wrong door and then sneaked off to find the linesman and get some gum. Hoddle went ballistic, and I shouted back at him, saying he was treating us like a school kid. It wasn't me smartest move, so in Rome I was on best behaviour.

The game against the Italians went well. I did exactly what I had been instructed to do and worked really hard. I got subbed with a few minutes to go, so I was on the bench next to Hoddle when the whistle went for full time. We both leapt in the air, we were so excited. The nil-all draw meant we had done it. I felt close to the manager then and confident I was in with a good shout of making it to me second World Cup. Dream on, Paul.

SKEWERED

Following our qualification, England had a series of friendly matches as we prepared for the World Cup. I played against Cameroon and Saudi Arabia at Wembley and then in May 1998 Hoddle took us off for a mini tournament in Morocco.

A day or so before we left for North Africa I appeared on Chris Evans' TV show and afterwards we went out for a few beers. And it really was just a few. Towards the end of the evening, I am not sure exactly what time, we were hungry and stopped for a chicken kebab. I thought it was about 11.30 p.m. but it might have been later. Chris reckons it was nearer 1.30 a.m.

Whatever time it was I know for certain we weren't drunk and a chicken kebab is hardly a deep-fried Mars bar, is it? And it is not as if I was the only player who was out that

We were strong and determined in our preparations for the World Cup.

evening. I know for a fact a whole bunch of the lads were in Soho getting bladdered, but they didn't get any stick for it. Anyway, we had our kebab and headed home but someone spotted us and took a photo that appeared in the papers.

Is that my England career I see disappearing into the distance?

Hoddle went mad, saying how he was worried about me eating habits, and questioning whether I was in a proper state to play for England. The whole incident was blown out of all proportion as far as I was concerned, but it left a nasty taste in the mouth. So it was against the backdrop of the shock revelation that English footballers sometimes eat foreign food (which to me was the only real story), that we headed off to Morocco where we were due to play the hosts and Belgium, before heading to La Manga in Spain for the final squad selection. Despite Hoddle's reaction, I still felt positive and confident that I would be going to France.

I played the full ninety minutes against Morocco, where Michael Owen scored his first England goal and was picked again for the game against Belgium. During the match I took a knock on the head and had to be bandaged up. As I was getting seen to my

mind drifted back almost nine years, to Terry Butcher on the treatment table after playing Sweden. It made me think how much playing for England meant to me.

I got on with the match but just after half-time I picked up a dead leg and was subbed. Sitting on the bench I could sense something wasn't right. I can't explain it, but I was overcome with this feeling of sadness. There was a voice inside us telling us I'd played me final game for England. I didn't want to believe it. How could that be true? I still had so much to give.

LA MANGA

I had got over me moment of doubt by the time we reached Spain. The atmosphere was upbeat, the training fun and I truly believed we had the right blend of youth and experience, grit and flair, to go one better than the last World Cup England had played in. I was certain I'd be part of it.

There was one moment when perhaps Walter Smith's words should have started to ring alarm bells in me head. La Manga was full of English ex-pats and holiday-makers. They were excited to have the squad there and wanted to say hello and wish us well. I was walking up the road alongside Hoddle when a group of them approached and asked me for my autograph. Only mine. I don't think he liked that much.

Even with that slightly awkward moment, we were all getting along well and the night before the final squad was to be announced there was a bit of a sing song. Everyone was there, having a few drinks and a laugh. At about one in the morning, Dave Seaman and Paul Ince put me to bed. I admit I was a touch unsteady on me feet, but who wasn't? Next morning when I woke up I wandered downstairs and asked how the night had gone

Football was the only thing on my mind at La Magna.

after I'd bailed out. Seems some of the boys were still up at four, drinking and carrying on.

I am going to race through what happened next, not because I am ashamed of it but because it isn't exactly a highlight of me football career. That morning we'd been told to do our own thing, but when I came across some of the lads lined up in a corridor I discovered that Hoddle was speaking to each of the players individually, at a set time. I thought that was a ridiculous way to treat professional footballers. It was like someone had been naughty at school and the headmaster was trying to find out who it was.

I got quite worked up about it, the hanging around and not knowing, so I went looking for someone to speak to and found a room where the England coaches, Glenn Roeder, Ray Clemence and John Gorman were sitting. 'What the fuck is going on? Is he really picking the squad like this?' I looked directly at Glenn, who has been a great friend to me for many years, and I saw a tear in his eye. That's the moment I knew I'd been dropped.

I ran out of the room, down the corridor and two-footed Hoddle's door. Phil Neville was in there. He didn't hang around when I started giving it everything I had. 'I can't fucking believe it. I can't believe you are doing this to me.' I kicked his wardrobe, threw over a table and smashed his lamp. In fairness to Hoddle, every time he said, 'Let me explain', I just shouted back at him, 'I don't want to talk to you. I don't want you to explain.' I wouldn't let him say a word to us. Eventually Paul Ince and Dave Seaman came in the room with a doctor and he gave us a Valium to calm me down.

As I was being taken to me room I remember Hoddle saying, 'Paul, you've got to go home now.' I had one last go at him. 'I don't have to do a fucking thing you tell me. I am out the World Cup. I'm free to do what the fuck I want. I'm not going home. I'm staying here!' I knew I couldn't, of course, and I didn't really want to, but equally I didn't want to go back to England. I was too embarrassed. I just wanted to escape. I couldn't face the press.

Eventually I got on the plane with the other guys who were kicked out. The next day I called Bryan Robson and tried to explain the situation. I was at Middlesbrough by then and Bryan said something that has stuck with me to this day. 'I can't believe he did that Paul, but the World Cup will be over soon, forgotten about one way or the other. Football will carry on. You just need to get yourself sorted and ready to play again.' He was right.

I still can't really understand why Hoddle didn't pick me. He blamed it on my eating and drinking but I felt fit and in good shape. The only explanation that makes sense to me is that it was his way of making a name for himself, just like Walter had said he would. I felt he wanted the World Cup to be all about him and not the players.

Do I hold a grudge against Glenn Hoddle for the decision he made? Not at all. What happened, happened. I've moved on with my life and so has he. We've met since and it has been fine. There is no room in my life for resentment. It achieves nothing.

CHAPTER 14

WRAPPING
IT UP

MIDDLESBROUGH AND EVERTON:
MARCH 1998 – MARCH 2002

BORO

As I said, I hadn't wanted to leave Rangers but it was clear from what was happening at Ibrox and in me personal life that my time in Glasgow had come to a natural end. Walter was on the move, a new manager was coming in and although the Rangers' chairman David Murray made it clear he didn't want me to go, there was a good offer on the table from a club that held a lot of appeal. Middlesbrough were on the up, they were League Cup finalists and chasing promotion to the Premiership. And from my point of view, the most important factor was that Bryan Robson was the manager.

Bryan had made it clear that he wanted a quick decision. With all that was going on at Middlesbrough he was looking to strengthen his squad immediately and needed to know whether I'd be joining him. But even still, the pull of Rangers was strong and I remained undecided.

I needed to speak to Bryan in person, so I drove down to the Riverside. Halfway there I started to cry. I kept thinking that if I just turned around now, drove back up the road, it would all be okay. It was a fantasy though, I knew that. There was no going back.

When I arrived Bryan had the contract there, ready for me to sign. I repeatedly made excuses, disappearing out to the toilet and the like, to delay the inevitable. But of course I eventually put pen to paper and for an instant it felt as though me heart was breaking, but only for a moment. I remembered that Boro had been the first club I'd had a proper trial for, a thousand years ago, and somehow it felt right to be coming full circle. And then there was Bryan's enthusiasm and excitement at what the club were looking to achieve. It was infectious and very quickly I was swept up in it all.

Paul Merson and Andy Townsend were there at the time, so I wasn't walking into a dressing room of complete strangers, which also helped. And the club itself was in great shape – a well-run academy producing real talent; a modern gym; fabulous training pitches. Basically everything you could want. That was all thanks to the chairman, who had put a lot of money in, but looking back I wonder if some of the squad began to take things for granted. During me time there I had this nagging feeling that, although the gaffer was pushing them hard and doing a good job, the players weren't quite hungry enough. Perhaps it was just too comfortable.

HIGHS AND LOWS AT BORO

S uch reflections on the team's mentality were way into the future. Of more immediate concern in March 1998 was the showdown with Chelsea. Bryan said he would play me in the cup final, and while I was excited at the prospect, I did feel a bit guilty about it. I hadn't contributed to getting there and the gaffer dropped Craig Hignett, a crowd favourite, to make room for me on the bench. Regardless of that though, when I got on I was still determined to do my very best. The truth was, however, that I hadn't had time to adjust to the fast pace of Chelsea's Premiership play. I

was struggling to find space to make me mark, not helped by the fact that Dennis Wise followed us all over the park, niggling away at me at every opportunity. I liked Wisey but he was a shit to play against.

I was also up against the brilliance of Gianfranco Zola. I knew him from me days at Lazio, when he was at Napoli, and as a sign of affection I learned the Italian for 'horse head' so I could call him something nice and friendly on the pitch. I reminded him of this during the match. I don't think he was too impressed. We had a bit of a set-to but afterwards it was fine. He's a quality bloke.

Middlesbrough lost 2–0 in extra time and with that result went me last chance to walk up those Wembley steps a winner. After the match, in the dressing room, I gave me medal to Craig Hignett. He deserved it much more than I did. On the final whistle, I was walking round the pitch, applauding the fans and thinking about my career and my new start when I looked up into the stands and there was a group of the Rangers players coming down to see us. Goram, McCall, Durranty, Durie, Ian Ferguson. Coisty too, I think. I hadn't known they were there. They'd come to wish us luck and say goodbye properly. That meant a lot to me. It said there were no hard feelings and that I had made the right decision.

After the final, the focus was fully on trying to secure promotion. As so often happens, there was a bit of a hangover from the cup exploits and we lost the next two league matches, but after that we put together a brilliant run of six unbeaten games to finish second. As our elevation to the Premiership became a distinct possibility with each passing result, people started saying that I was past it and would never cope with the top flight. That spurred us on. I got stuck in and we started to rip some of the teams apart. It was a fantastic run and I loved it. I was ready to take on the big boys again.

My first steps in the Premiership with Middlesbrough. Leeds at home.

'October 1998 proved a dark time for me. Too much drink
led to a three-week stint in the Priory but I was back for
this match against Forest at the start of November.
The welcome I received was incredible. Thank you.'

A week later I scored a twenty-five-yard free kick in our 3–3 draw away to Southampton. My best game for Boro so far. I'd found my feet in the Premiership and I was happy.

February 2000 and a daft tussle with Villa's George Boateng results in me breaking my arm. The beginning of the end at Middlesbrough.

THE TOFFEES

Bryan Robson was great at Middlesbrough. He looked after me and in my view he was a brilliant manager. But even he couldn't stop the train wreck that was Paul Gascoigne as my days at the club became numbered. I was going through a bleak period of my life, drinking too much and not enjoying my football. The broken arm I sustained after clattering into Boateng kept me out for six weeks and although I did recover, it was clear I needed to move on.

I booked into a health farm to try and sort meself out and then I did the only thing I could think of that would properly help me. I rang Walter Smith at Everton. 'Walter, you remember I did you a favour once, leaving Lazio to come to Rangers for less money? Well, I really need you to help me now.'

Archie Knox had gone to Everton with Walter and I met the two of them to discuss a possible move on a free transfer. They asked if everything was okay with me and I promised them it was, so they agreed to think about it. The next thing I knew, the deal was going through and I was buzzing again. I was sure I had at least two good years left at the top and I was desperate to repay their belief in me. The squad were heading off to Italy for pre-season training and I was left behind in Liverpool to complete the necessary fitness tests and sign the deal. With the paperwork finalised, I followed a few days later and almost immediately on arrival at the camp, Walter hauled me into his office.

'I can't believe I have signed you. I can't believe what I've done. Your tests have come back and your system is full of alcohol.' He wanted to throw us out of the club there and then before I'd even kicked a ball. He wouldn't speak to us for three days and I couldn't blame him. I'd screwed up big time…again. I'd given me word that I was clean and it was a lie.

I begged for a second chance. I was ashamed of meself and I worked me nuts off for the next week to try and prove their faith in me hadn't been misplaced. At the end of the training camp Walter and Archie called me in for a final showdown. 'Okay Paul, we've been talking and we think we've got the Gazza back that we wanted.' I can't describe the relief and the gratitude I felt towards them.

It was the start of a new phase for me – back with Walter and Archie, experienced players around me, captains from other clubs alongside quality youngsters coming through. After having let everything slip at Boro I was focused on football again and loving it.

HIGHS AND LOWS AT EVERTON

That first season started pretty well. It took me a few games to get my fitness back up to Premiership levels but I managed it and was beginning to play well and make a real contribution. The fans were fantastic, giving me a brilliant reception every time, even when I was on the bench. They used to hand us loads of the Everton toffees which I would happily munch away on while watching the game. Mind you, I did suffer a bit when I went out for a warm-up along the touchline – the toffees used to give us a terrible stitch sometimes. I kept that quiet from the gaffer. Best not to worry him, I thought.

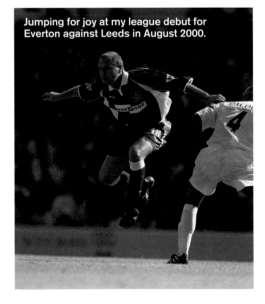
Jumping for joy at my league debut for Everton against Leeds in August 2000.

November 2001: back from Arizona, fitter than I'd been in a long time, and back amongst the goals against Bolton.

So everything was going well until a series of injuries towards the end of the year kept me out for three months, and then when I was back my form, and the team's, dropped off. The old worries and upsets came back and I turned once again to drink to try and hide from it all. By the end of the season, Walter had had enough and gave me an ultimatum. 'You have two options, Paul. Get the fuck out of this club or get to rehab. If you have the balls to do it, do it.' I respected him too much not to listen to his warning and agreed to go to a clinic in Arizona over the summer to try and sort myself out once and for all.

I returned from the States clean, healthy, full of energy and looking forward to the new season. But my bright start didn't last. Not long after I scored against Bolton, I had more trouble with me hernia, then tore a muscle. I kept off the booze during this layoff but my head wasn't right. I was miserable and desperately low.

We were due to play Sunderland at home on 12 January 2002. I had a load of mates who were Sunderland supporters and they kept calling to tell us that Gavin McCann was going to piss all over us in the match the next day. They were just winding us up, but it got to me. I guess it was the excuse I had been looking for. I was with Jimmy at the time and asked him to nip out and get four bottles of wine. He wasn't happy about it, but I insisted.

That night I drank three and a half of the bottles, took eleven sleeping tablets, woke up at 6 a.m. with the shakes, took a couple more tablets, finished off the wine, fell back asleep, woke up again 9 a.m., had a treble brandy, another sleeping tablet, a smoke, and went to the game. I was in a terrible state, shaking badly, so I had another treble brandy, took another tablet and went out on the pitch and played a blinder. Afterwards, I went straight home and fell asleep.

Man of the Match, so I am told.

Next morning I asked Jimmy how I had done. 'Look at the table,' he said, pointing to a big bottle of champagne. 'You won Man of the Match.'

It is hard to call that match a highlight, even though I played well, because it marked the start of yet another decline. My days at the very top of football, where I had been for going on seventeen years, were drawing to a close. The end arrived in inglorious fashion with a 3–0 FA Cup quarter-final defeat at Middlesbrough. Walter was sacked three days later and I never kicked a ball in the Premiership again.

Goodbye and thank you. For everything.

My career started with a ball when I was seven and I've had one ever since.

I wouldn't change anything in my football life, not on the playing side of things. Yeah, okay, maybe a couple of rash challenges leading to injuries, which robbed me of more years than I like to think about, and certainly the drinking, no question about that, but in terms of football and the decisions I made? I wouldn't change any of them.

Writing this book has allowed me to look back over the years and I've been happy with what I've seen. It has made me a bit sad at times, I must admit, wishing it was all still going on, wishing I was still out there, with the roar of the crowd, the banter in the changing rooms and the moments of pure joy at doing things on the pitch that no one else could do. But at least I have done all these things once. That'll do me.

When people say that I wasted my talent I always think, why don't you come around and look at me trophies and me medals and me headlines? I know I had a great career, no one can say otherwise. I've got an FA Youth Cup medal, an FA Cup medal, a World Cup medal, a European Championship medal, I was voted BBC Sports Personality of the Year, I won awards for North East Player of the Month and Year, I was PFA Young Player of the Year, Scottish Football Writers' Player of the Year, Scottish Players' Player of the Year, I've got two Scottish League medals, a Scottish Cup medal and a Scottish League Cup medal. Not bad.

One day I'll get them all out, polish them up and put them on display. I'll invite the Queen to come and have a look. If she's forgiven me for trying to kiss Diana, that is.

I think back to that bairn from Dunston, kicking a tennis ball around, and then I look at the photographs in this book and there is only one word for that journey. Well, two, actually – fucking unbelievable.

It has been a joy and a privilege. Thank you for sharing it with me. Cheers. x

ACKNOWLEDGEMENTS

The Providence Project in Bournemouth made this book possible. Wait, that's not right, it was the people there who made it possible. Without their support I could never have done it. Thank you all, and in particular Steve Spiegel, Carole Spiegel, Paul Spanjar and Daryle Fortescue, along with Doughie, Darren, Garanz, Gary, Clinton, Duncan, Steve F, Sarah, Lisa, John, Cheryl and Anita and everyone who works there. You have all been brilliant.

I'd also like to thank all the players and managers I've worked with over the years. There would be no stories to tell without you lot.

To everyone at Simon & Schuster, thank you for having faith that someone might want to read about me football, and especially to Kerr MacRae, Rhea Halford, Rory Scarfe, Leigh Ann Broadbent, Jo Edgecombe and Anna Robinson for helping make it all happen.

Big thanks also to Dave Wilson who spent so much time travelling down to see me to produce such an amazing book. Cheers mate.

Most of all though, I want to say thank you to Mam, Dad, Anna, Carl and Lindsay and my nephews Cameron, Jay and Joe and my nieces Harley and Lauren. I hope you know what you all mean to me.

Enjoy the book.

Gazza X

PICTURE CREDITS

Action Images
43, 60, 91 (Above), 93, 98, 122, 138, 139 (Below), 141, 173, 174, 178 (Above), 194, 209, 210 (Above and Below), 211, 212 (Above), 216, 220, 221, 234, 244 (Below), 245, 246, 247, 248

Colorsport
30, 42 (Above), 44 (Below), 47, 49, 54 (Below), 74 (Above), 79, 96, 104 (Below), 109, 110 (Above Left and Below Right), 118 (Above), 130 (Above and Below), 155, 164 (Below), 217, 226, 228, 231, 232, 253

Corbis
94, 103 (Below Right)

Getty
29, 33, 38, 41, 42 (Below), 48, 66, 89, 91 (Below), 105, 110 (Middle), 113, 116, 129 (Above and Below), 132–3, 140 (Below), 149, 150, 163 (Above), 181, 182 (Top and Bottom), 183, 184, 186–7, 189, 192, 198, 199 (Middle and Below Right), 201 (Above), 202 (Above and Below), 233, 238

Mirrorpix
26, 28, 31, 34, 35, 37, 45 (Above and Below), 46, 50, 54 (Above), 55 (Above and Below), 56 (Above), 57 (Above), 58, 59, 61 (Above and Below), 62, 64–5, 72, 76, 82, 83, 85, 102, 112, 115, 119, 124, 125, 127 (Above), 131, 134, 140 (Above), 143 (Above and Below), 145 (Below), 158, 159 (Above and Below), 162, 165, 196, 204, 207, 213 (Right and Left), 223, 235 (Above)

NI Syndication
53, 235 (Middle), 235 (Below)

North News
12

Press Association
19, 21, 22, 27, 32 (Below), 56 (Below), 69, 70–1, 74 (Below), 75, 77, 80, 88, 90, 97, 123 (Below), 128, 136, 139 (Above), 144, 145 (Above), 153, 154, 156, 157, 160, 161, 163 (Below), 164 (Above), 167, 169, 170, 177, 178 (Below), 179, 185, 190, 195, 200, 201 (Below), 203, 212 (Below), 214, 215, 219, 224–5, 236, 237, 240, 242, 243, 249

Rex Features
57 (Below, Below Right Top and Bottom), 78, 84, 108, 117, 120, 123 (Above), 126, 137 (Above and Below), 172, 229, 241, 244 (Above)

Well Offside
32 (Above), 44 (Above), 73, 99, 104 (Above), 107, 114, 118 (Below), 127 (Below), 146, 230 (Above and Below), 250

Pages 7–8 (Top to Bottom, Left to Right)
Mirrorpix; Action Images; Well Offside; Well Offside; Press Association; Mirrorpix; Action Images; Colorsport